D1127387

RUNNING IN THE RED

SUNY Series on Urban Public Policy
Mark Schneider and Richard C. Rich, Editors

RUNNING IN THE RED

The Political Dynamics
of Urban Fiscal Stress

Irene S. Rubin

NORTHERN ILLINOIS UNIVERSITY

State University of New York Press
Albany

To Boo, who gave up his turn on the wordprocessor so that this book could be completed.

Published by State University of New York Press, Albany

© 1982 State University of New York

Printed in the United States of America

For information, address State University of New York Press, State University Plaza, Albany, N.Y. 12246

Library of Congress Cataloging in Publication Data

Rubin, Irene.
  Running in the red.

  (SUNY series on urban public policy)
  Bibliography: p. 159
  Includes index.
    1. Municipal finance—United States. 2. Municipal government—United States. I. Title. II. Series.
  HJ9145.R8   352.1′0973   81-9329
  ISBN 0-87395-564-1   AACR2
  ISBN 0-87395-565-X (pbk.)

Contents

Tables

Acknowledgments

I would like to thank the elected officials and city staff of Southside for their time and for permission to do the study; I hope they find the study useful. I would also like to thank Herbert Rubin, Charles Levine, Terry Clark, and Gerry Suttles, all of whom have read the manuscript at various stages and made helpful, critical comments. Thanks are due also to James Conway who provided research assistance, particularly on the section dealing with the city's response to the riot in 1968.

One

Urban Financial Stress

On December 10, 1975, the American Enterprise Institute for Public Policy Research held a roundtable discussion entitled "The Financial Crisis of our Cities."[1] Melvin Laird was the moderator, and the guest panelists were Governor Hugh Carey of New York, Senator Jacob Javits of New York, Sidney Jones from the U.S. Treasury Department, and Senator Charles Percy of Illinois. The discussion began with some consensus on the causes of urban fiscal stress, and the effects of federal highway programs and mortgage insurance in hastening the exodus out of the central city. But the discussion soon turned to the differences between Chicago and New York City. Senator Percy claimed that the stable, fiscally conservative leadership which Mayor Daley gave Chicago was the real difference. Senator Javits argued that New Yorkers' hearts were bigger than their pocketbooks, whereas Chicago's fiscal solvency was at the price of unmet social needs. Percy argued that Daley controlled the unions, while New York's political leaders did not. Governor Carey countered that Percy's background was not political—that he had come from industry and had a great belief in private enterprise. Most of the rest of the discussion revolved around the devolution of functions and costs from cities to states and to the federal government and around the implications for equity in various solutions.

This roundtable discussion highlights the fact that urban fiscal stress has raised questions of values. How much money should taxation give to the poor? How broad in scope should the public sector be? What should be the relationship between the state, the federal government, and the cities? These questions turn on the issue of causation. Did the migrations of poor blacks to the cities of the Northeast and Midwest cause the fiscal crisis? Was it reallocation to the poor which raised taxes and chased out businesses and the upper and middle classes, causing the decline in tax base? Were cities trying to provide too many services that should have been provided by the private sector? Were the cities profligate, corrupt, inept, too generous to interest groups and the poor? Or were the cities victims of national or regional trends over which they had no control, such as unionization, migration, inflation, recession, industrial location, and old age?

If services to the poor really caused fiscal stress, then there might be an argument for reducing such services. If, however, the cities have largely ignored the poor and left their care to the state and federal government, or if they have spent as much or more on other special interests or on protecting the rich against the poor, the fairness and wisdom of cutting back services to the poor must be questioned.

If the causes of fiscal stress are national in scope, and if some cities are bearing the burden for other cities and the countryside, then the unfairness of making each city go it alone could be remedied by a policy of federal intervention and aid. If, on the other hand, the causes of fiscal stress are local and controllable, a national policy would have serious negative consequences. There is an inherent unfairness in asking the general population to pay for the mistakes or problems of a few cities. Secondly, federal money will be wasted if the same practices that created fiscal stress continue without reform. Furthermore, many cities will surrender their autonomy to the federal government in exchange for no compensating value.

Given the dimensions and import of proposed solutions to the fiscal crisis, the question of causes takes on new meaning. This book is an attempt to get behind the rhetoric to describe the development of financial problems in one case study city.

We assume that the case study city is typical of many other cities experiencing fiscal stress. We know that many other American cities are in trouble. In a study done in 1976, eight out of fifty-two American cities were experiencing symptoms of fiscal stress that showed up in the census.[2] Since there is a tendency to suppress bad financial news, the actual picture was probably worse. Moreover, the situation does not appear to be a passing phase, but a chronic problem for many cities. Taxpayers' revolts across the country suggest that the problem may be getting worse.

Financial stress involves a reduction in the number of financial options available to a city. It frequently implies a higher cost for the available options. A larger proportion of the budget becomes nondiscretionary. The narrowing of options may result from mandated programs, high debt service, labor contracts, civil service type personnel systems, increase in tax effort, and/or a relative imbalance of revenue and expenditure which may be caused by inflation or recession. Bouts of fiscal stress may be characterized by cash flow problems, by short-term borrowing, either internally or externally, or by deficits. Fiscal stress need not necessarily end in default or bankruptcy. but it has the potential to do so.[3]

The consequences of urban financial stress are enormous. In practical terms, stress increases the cost of borrowing, the proportion of the budget spent on debt service, and the cost of goods and services because the cheapest vendors will not deal with an organization that does not pay its bills on time. Within the city government, more power may shift to the budget director as the gap widens between authorized expenditures and actual revenues. Political alliances may fall apart as resources which hold them together vanish. Some interest groups may decline in strength as others grow; fiscally conservative business groups are likely to increase control, while social service agencies and unions are apt to be curtailed. Service levels may drop. Both layoffs, with consequent loss of sunk costs of recruitment and training, and hiring and purchasing freezes may occur, with their attendant irra-tionalities. Policies of laying off personnel by seniority may result both in discrimination against women and minorities and in an aging and inflexible work force. The depletion of reserve funds can turn unex-pected expenses into major headaches. Running a city in deficit is both more difficult and more expensive than running a fiscally sound city.

There are, then, several good reasons for doing a case study of a city in fiscal stress. Many cities are experiencing such stress, and they are changing in ways we do not yet understand. This case study should provide both some insight into those changes and a more neutral point of departure for exploring the major issues raised in the New York City debate, including the relative importance of migrations of the poor, tax base erosion, and political structure and leadership. The case study should also alert us to possible sources of variation be-tween cities experiencing fiscal stress by providing a comparison with the model of New York City.

The Case Study City

The case study city, which will be called Southside,[4] was selected for the study because it was experiencing deficits and was engaged in cutbacks and layoffs in 1976. The city is middle-sized, with a popula-tion of about seventy-five thousand, and is probably similar in some ways to many aging industrial cities in the Midwest. The city maintains only a limited number of functions in its budget. It can be described as both a "blue collar community"[5] and a reformed city. The apparent contradiction between these two descriptions is suggestive of the city's political culture.

Visually, the city is old and somewhat dilapidated, especially on its east side. Potholes and patched streets suggest fiscal stress and policies of piecemeal repair. Extensive suburbanization followed by annexation has extended the west side, much of which is newer, less dense, and richer than the east side. With the settlement of blacks and Hispanics on the east side, the cultural split between the two sections has been further exaggerated.

Economic, social, and political factors interacted over time in Southside to create a fiscal crisis. Black migration to the city at a time when its economy could not absorb them caused black family income to lag behind white family income. White prejudice combined with low black income to restrict blacks to several deteriorating areas of the central city, and hold down assessed valuations and growth in property tax yields in those neighborhoods. Development of black ghettos accelerated white exodus from the city, with the result that the city, at great cost in services, annexed the surrounding white suburbs to recapture its tax base.

The city's narrow scope of services meant that it could not respond to the influx of poor by increasing social services. These were either performed by other units of government or not performed at all. The city's primary response to the riots in black neighborhoods after Martin Luther King's assassination was to increase expenditures on police, often without increasing revenue to cover the increased costs. Thus the city's racial polarization contributed directly to the deficits.

That a conservative city manager government ran deficits is problematic to students of local government. City manager government, with its antipatronage, anti-interest group bias and its emphasis on efficiency, is supposed to avoid waste and provide better service for the dollar. If the city manager government was effective, then being efficient, antipatronage and anti-interest groups was not enough to prevent fiscal stress.

Why a city manager government ran deficits is a question of particular concern in this book. In the course of the study, I found several explanations. First, political and social conservatism of a particular brand became too dominant in the city. Politicians were reluctant to look for new revenues or to raise taxes when necessary, and their reluctance to borrow for capital needs accelerated the rate of physical decline and encouraged disinvestment. City government responded to a rapidly growing minority population and to increased poverty and increased crime with more and better paid police.[6] Costs thus increased beyond inflation while no new revenues were generated.

A second factor was that city manager government was never completely achieved. The particular compromises between reformed and unreformed government which characterized the city were not financially stable. Thirdly, the city responded to windfall revenues from the federal government by spending them on operating expenses to satisfy demands growing out of social cleavages. After the initial period of revenue growth, the city was left with increasing operating costs and stabilizing levels of revenue. Each of these explanations is discussed in the study.

The Literature on Urban Fiscal Stress

Before detailing events in the case study city, it is appropriate to describe the literature on urban fiscal stress, and to suggest what kind of contribution the study will make to that literature.

There is a considerable body of empirical literature on urban fiscal stress, but it tends to be fragmented, nontheoretical, and lacking in consensus. For example, many authors have tried to define fiscal stress and measure its extent. There are nearly as many definitions as authors, and, not surprisingly, there is little consensus on how widespread fiscal stress is.[7] A number of authors have looked at various causes of increased expenditures or decreased revenues, but again, the results have been piecemeal and difficult to aggregate.[8] With the exception of a few mathematical models,[9] the literature generally ignores possible interactions of different causes of fiscal stress over time.

If much of the empirical work lacks theoretical focus, it is not because there are no theories to explain fiscal stress. The literature on urban fiscal stress can be viewed in terms of three different but related theoretical approaches:[10] the migration/tax base erosion argument, the growth-of-bureaucracy argument, and the political vulnerability model. Each of these positions is a loose grouping of related themes. Each also generates a distinctive set of recommendations for eliminating fiscal stress.

Migrations and Tax Base Erosion

The first thesis is that population migrations are the basic cause of urban fiscal strain. There are really three separate models which fit into this category. The first is that migrations of poor blacks and Hispanics to the Northeast, Midwest, and far West create new demands on city government which exceed the capacities of cities. These demands include education, welfare, job training, and health.[11]

The second migration model refers to the exodus of people and jobs from the central city to the suburbs. Since it is the middle and upper classes who leave (this much has been empirically documented), the central cities are left with a higher percentage of poor, who presumably need (consume) more services than the middle and upper classes. The central city has less revenue with which to supply these needs, since the middle and upper classes have left the city and some businesses have followed them. Some authors add a negative feedback loop, in which the exodus of some taxpayers puts a higher burden on those remaining, who then leave, accelerating the rate of departure. A related argument in the literature on suburbanization and fiscal stress is that the newly created suburban governments take fiscal advantage of the central city by using its facilities without paying for them. Police protection, for example, is provided to commuters who do not pay for it.[12]

The third population argument refers to the shift from the snowbelt to the sunbelt. This shift implies a net decline in population of a whole metropolitan area. Such declines are based on structural changes in the economy that make a whole region less economically competitive. Some of the decline may be attributed to increased urban congestion and resultant high rents, time consuming transportation, pollution, and the like. Some of the decline may result from a change in technology which no longer offers as many economic advantages for locating in or near the central business district. Finally, some of the shift may result from differential factor costs besides rentals—higher labor costs and higher prices for electricity or gasoline. Whatever the causes, the results are a net reduction in jobs, loss of population, and the erosion of the tax base.[13]

Although all three arguments seem related, they have been developed separately, as each trend became clear, and each has generated a different set of solutions to fiscal stress. Those who argue that demands of the poor are the problem have urged spinoff of functions to other levels of government. The poor, they contend, are not the responsibility of individual cities; equal benefits across states and between cities would eliminate the motivation to move to a city with higher welfare, and would also eliminate the motivation to stay in a city because of its benefits instead of looking for jobs elsewhere. Uniformity of welfare would have several advantages: it would put the burden on everyone, not just a few cities; it would be paid for by a highly elastic source of revenue; it would increase the mobility of the poor and hence reduce unemployment and poverty itself. Some theorists also believe that if cities were to stop taxing the rich to give to the poor, they would slow down the flow of outward migration to low tax areas.

Theorists concerned with suburbanization as a source of fiscal stress tend to favor metropolitan government, or short of that, sharing the costs of city services with suburbanites. Annexation of more land is sometimes part of the recommended solution.

Interregional migration, the newest of the models, has not generated a fixed set of solutions. A deterministic theme runs through this literature. Old cities are too confined for new industries, factor costs are too high, political systems are too rigid to deal with change. While economic activity may eventually cycle back to the Northeast and Midwest, these areas are in a phase of decline to which perhaps an adjustment must be made. Some cities may have grown larger than their economies can sustain.[14] Those who believe that cities can do little about economic base erosion frequently call upon the federal government to rescue the cities or at least to soften the pangs of decline.[15]

Bureaucratic Growth

The second perspective on urban financial problems grows out of the Public Choice School, which deals with nonmarket economics. The major tenet of this school of thought is that government has grown too large too rapidly. While some of this growth has occurred because of increased demand for services for which citizens are willing to pay, part of the growth has also stemmed from other causes for which citizens are unwilling to pay. The theoretical reasons for excessive governmental growth are varied.

Public Choice theorists hold that in the public sector the individual will demand too many services since increased quantities are not regulated by increased costs. This is particularly true where all citizens pay to benefit a few. These few have managed to share the costs of what they want among the citizenry, which makes services so cheap that their demands for them increase. Since every person or group can hope to get such "cheap" services, all push up demands. The results are an excessively large demand and an overgrown, overly expensive government.

A second mechanism sometimes proposed by Public Choice theorists is the power of bureaucrats and elected officials. The motivation of such people is assumed to be self-interest, and the assumption is made that politicians in particular are sufficiently free of citizen control to try to realize personal benefits. Bureaucrats' ends will always be served by a larger bureaucracy, which typically provides higher salaries. Because bureaucrats have the power and the interest to vote, they always vote in favor of expansion. The larger the bureaucracy, the more votes it has, and the more power it has to expand itself. In this model, government employment should constantly increase.

A related model offers that those who benefit from a government program will always want to increase their benefits. The more people receive such benefits the greater the demand for higher benefit levels. This model accelerates at an increasing rate. Some argue, however, that there may be an equilibrium point; that is, the greater the benefits the greater the opposition to the program from nonrecipients and the weaker the demand from the beneficiaries, since increased benefits have less value than the original.[16]

The solutions proposed by the Public Choice theorists include (1) returning to the market those functions inappropriate to the public sector in order to let demand be regulated by price (contracting out); (2) increasing the incidence of user fees, so people associate their increased demands with increased costs; and (3) keeping the size of government units small so that demands for services and costs to the individual are felt simultaneously. With respect to bureaucratic expansion per se, one solution is to deny government employees the right to vote.

Political Vulnerability

The third general theory of fiscal stress concerns itself with the vulnerability of city hall to demands. Simply put, the argument is that the more vulnerable city hall is to demands the greater the likelihood of fiscal stress. There are three related models, one concerned with the collapse of voter coalitions as a source of political vulnerability, a second concerned with structural weaknesses in the form of government, and a third concerned with the structure and powers of interest groups.

In the first of these political vulnerability models, a mayor who has a large plurality he can always count on is in a position to refuse demands if necessary. If, on the other hand, he cannot seem to put together a coalition and is desperately trying to put one together by appealing to a variety of groups, he is likely to overspend. In a nonreformed city, this additional expenditure may result in an increase in patronage hiring. In a more reformed setting, where patronage is more sharply curtailed, the attempt to rebuild coalitions may be reflected in the use of bureaucracy to deliver minor favors to citizens who request such attention. Or certain neighborhoods may receive more or better services than other neighborhoods.

Fiscal stress is thus seen in terms of waxing and waning coalitions of voters. It is a cyclical or at least a recurring phenomenon, but it eventually cures itself—coalitions are rebuilt and less money is required to sustain than to build coalitions. The most recent phase of fiscal stress was caused by the migrations of poor blacks to the northern cities and by the exodus of whites from the central cities. Combined, these two population changes broke down coalitions which had supported politicians, and new coalitions had to be forged at greater cost than the cities could afford.[17]

The second model of political vulnerability addresses the form of the city government. Its argument is that machine and strong-mayor governments are more responsive to, yet more vulnerable to, demands than reformed city manager governments. The whole ideology of the reformed government movement suggests that city manager government will deliver more services more efficiently than machine government, though not at an absolutely lower level of dollar expenditures. The budgetary control of the city manager should insulate the budget from political concerns. The idea that poor management caused fiscal stress is prominent in business circles; the idea that business management can save the cities is still part of the reform ideology.[18]

The third political vulnerability model is the interest group model. This model emphasizes the relative strength of competing interest groups. The argument is that the better organized and more active interest groups are, the more vulnerable city hall is to their demands. While much of the literature on urban interest groups has centered on the degree to which power is concentrated in a single or several interest groups or is dispersed to many occasionally active groups, the number of interest groups and the extent to which they express class interests has implications for fiscal policy as well.[19]

The remedies proposed by those emphasizing political vulnerability vary according to the particular submodel involved. If the problem is decline of voter coalitions due to in-migration and out-migration, then stabilization of the population combined with the coalition building activities of politicians should eliminate the problem. Bouts of fiscal stress will be followed by bouts of fiscal health. If the problem is structural weakness, the recommended solution is more reform. Finally, if interest group activity is diagnosed as the problem, then the recommended solution is the increased activation of those interest groups identified with limited spending strategies.

The Study in the Context of the Literature

What can we say about the literature on fiscal stress and the contribution of a case study at this time? First, the empirical work seems
fragmented and not well integrated into the theory. Secondly, while
the theory is broad and fairly well developed, there have been few
attempts to combine themes and observe their interactions over time.
It is clear that what is needed at present is a closer relationship between the theory and empirical work, as well as some sense of how
various causes combine in particular urban settings. This book represents a step in that direction. Propositions derived from the three
theoretical perspectives will be compared with events in the case
study city.

Since case study analysis is not generally useful for model testing,
what then can be said of the relationship between the case study and
the literature? First, the literature on urban fiscal stress provided an
intellectual framework that suggested gathering data on these elements: economic base erosion, migrations, bureaucratic growth, and
political structure and process. Secondly, there is a nice intellectual
tension between the case study narrative and the three somewhat
different approaches to the materials. The reader is invited to compare
the theory with the case study version as it unfolds. To facilitate this
comparison, each of the models has been broken down into propositions.

The first, described as the "Migration/Tax Base Erosion" model,
involves a negative cycle. The basic argument is as follows:

1.1. Fiscal stress is caused by tax base erosion which occurs
     while the city increases its outlays to service the poor.
1.2. As the tax base declines and service levels either remain
     constant or increase, tax rates will increase.
1.3. As tax rates increase, the tax burden on businesses and home-
     owners increases, and more businesses and middle- and
     upper-class residents leave the city, whose tax base is re-
     duced still further. The cycle then repeats.

Specific corollaries of this model are that the current round of urban
fiscal stress was caused by two factors:

1.4. Migrations of poor blacks and Hispanics to the central cities
     brought about an expansion of services aimed at the poor

which resulted in higher per capita expenditures. These services may be either of the public safety/sanitation type or of the social welfare/education variety—the model does not specify.

1.5. Businesses leave the central city for a variety of reasons, including high taxes, expensive labor, land, power or transportation, and changing technical requirements.

The second model is described as "Bureaucratic Expansion." It can be expressed in the following propositions:

2.1. One major cause of fiscal stress is that government performs the wrong functions: separable rather than collective goods are provided by the public sector, the beneficiaries of which increase demands for publicly provided services.

2.2. Taxpayers in general may be reluctant to pay additional taxes because (1) they see that other citizens benefit rather than they themselves or the public at large, or (2) they perceive that bureaucrats aggrandize themselves at public expense.

2.3. Bureaucrats always want to expand their bureaus, because (1) they measure their own prestige by the size of their bureaus and the number of their employees, and (2) they can improve their own salaries more easily in a large bureau than in a small one.

2.4. Bureaucrats have sufficient political control to bring about the expansion they desire. This exercise of power will accelerate public spending.

2.5. Just as some citizens increase demands for public sector services because of their low cost (that is, they have shared the cost with other citizens who did not benefit), so city governments will increase their demands for federal aid because it seems cheap to them. Federal funds will increase local expenditures, cause an increase in the scope of local government activities, and distort local priorities.

The "Political Vulnerability" model, the third of our series, has two versions, cyclical and noncyclical. The cyclical model has a built-in stabilizer.

3.1. A change in population composition, location, or voting preference breaks up stable voting coalitions among the electorate. Such a period is characterized by a plethora of small

factions and many competing candidates, each with only a
small following.

3.2. Money is expended by city government to cement a new
voter coalition. These expenditures may include an increase
in patronage jobs, the location of particular projects in particular neighborhoods, the award of city contracts to particular businessmen, the distribution of routine city services on
the basis of political loyalty, salary increases to organized
city employees, or the satisfaction of interest group demands.

3.3. Coalitions are built and expenditures decline.

The noncyclical version describes changes which cause increased
vulnerability to demands.

3.4. A change in governmental structure results in weaknesses in
the form of government or in the processes of administration
which make city hall vulnerable to demands.

3.5. An increase in the effective demands of interest groups results in greater governmental vulnerability to demands. The
increase may result from a changing population composition
(increased needs) or a more effective organization of interest
groups (demands).

The reader should be advised that clear information on every prop-
osition cannot be provided. In some cases the only available evidence was a subjective feeling or a chance remark. The greater emphasis on some propositions rather than others reflects not only the
availability of evidence, but also the author's preference for a theory
with a self-correcting mechanism rather than a theory of continuous
decline. This preference reflects a desire to help find solutions to
urban fiscal stress. Since Southside did get out of deficits by the end
of the study, this emphasis on self-correcting mechanisms seems jus-
tifiable.

Organization of The Book

The study began as an exploration of fiscal stress alone but broad-
ened into a study of economic, social, and political processes when it
became clear that budgets, audits, assessed values, and tax yields did
not provide all the answers. The organization of the book reflects this
idea of layering, of a continuing search for more and more pieces of

the puzzle.[20] The overall thrust of the book is to present a rich narrative
of how fiscal stress occurred, why it lasted as long as it did, and what
finally brought it to an end. The outcome should be not only a better
understanding of urban fiscal stress but also a better understanding of
the political system as it interacts with the economy and with social
change.

Chapter 2 relates the history and anatomy of the fiscal crisis in
Southside. This chapter describes the revenue and expenditure problems of the city and pinpoints them in the budget. Chapter 3 examines
the economic base erosion thesis by describing the pattern of growth
and decline in the city and the impact of migrations on city expenditures. Chapters 4 and 5 explore the political causes of fiscal stress,
with explanations for bureaucratic growth on one hand and political
vulnerability on the other. Chapter 6 puts together all the causes of
fiscal stress in several ways. First, it considers all the reasons for fiscal
stress given by different groups of actors at city hall and evaluates
their explanations in light of available evidence. Then it puts the
causes of fiscal stress in historical sequence. In chapter 7, the changes
made by the city are examined to see whether it really did recover
from fiscal stress by using its own resources. The concluding chapter
summarizes the study in terms of the strengths and weaknesses of the
propositions and adds to the existing theories the model of the self-
correcting city. It also demonstrates the probability that the conditions
found in Southside will also be present in other cities. The methodol-
ogy of the study is summarized in the appendix.

Two

Anatomy of the Fiscal Crisis

This chapter will relate the history of the deficits, how they were discovered, and what the city did to eliminate them. This description will include a budgetary analysis indicating where the deficits came from and how and why they occurred.

History of the Deficits

Publicly admitted deficits first occurred in 1972. The city manager reported that there had been hidden deficits in two of the previous four years. Later reconstructions estimated deficits of $270,000 and $440,000 for 1971 and 1972 respectively. The lobbyist for the downtown businessmen who had been present at finance committee meetings insisted in an interview that the city council knowingly passed deficit budgets but that no one at city hall had paid much attention to the deficits at that time.

The reason for this lack of attention is not clear. On the one hand, staff tended to minimize the size of deficits by sliding expenditures forward into the next fiscal year and by distorting budgets to make them look more balanced than they were in fact. It is not at all clear whether these subterfuges were matters of conscious self-protection, of ignorance or incompetence, or results of political pressure. On the other hand, councilmen claimed they mistakenly paid attention only to the bottom line, that is, gross revenues matched against gross expenditures, rather than to fund-by-fund accounting. In his 1971 and 1972 budget prefaces the city manager objected to the councilmen's indifference to budget details, but his view did not prevail at that stage.

As a result of councilmen's view of the deficits and the tendency of staff to minimize or hide the deficits, little action was taken during the early years of deficits. At the end of 1972, after a change in personnel, the new finance director "found" the deficits. In early 1973 there was a two-year plan to put the city back on its feet. The budget director left before this plan could be implemented, and the assistant city manager became the acting finance director. In an interview he reported that he found $4 million in deficits in 1974. Reflecting on his discovery, he commented, "It did not take long to figure out that we were borrowing and would prolong the deficit."

The deficits continued to grow through 1975 until a combination of circumstances outside city control prompted it to take action. When cutbacks occurred in early 1976, the unions accused the city management of gross ineptitude for continuing to hire new personnel in the face of a building crisis. The assistant city manager indicated that the city staff indeed had not forseen the need for drastic cuts. The city had been suffering with the consequences of stress for several years— cash flow problems, increased costs, and managerial reverberations— but these alone were insufficient to motivate changes.

Three outside events brought about a change of attitude. The first was the intervention of the state to halt pension underfunding. Cities all over the state were made to guarantee gradual improvement over twenty years. This action made public the city's practice of "borrowing" from its pension funds by reducing contributions below the level required by sound actuarial practice. The resulting increase in the cost of payments to pension funds made fiscal problems more acute.

The second event that riveted public attention upon the financial picture was a near default on water and sewer bonds. Money to pay off the bonds was supposed to come from an operating surplus but it was not available; so funds were temporarily diverted from another sewer and water account. This manner of averting a default raised issues of compliance with the bond ordinance establishing the Water and Sewer Department, which was forced to raise water rates to increase its operating revenue. Department heads and other officials speculated informally that interfund borrowing from the Water and Sewer Department was the cause of the near default, but they were quite careful not to mention this matter in public.[1] The city government at this point was pressed with two concerns: the politically unpopular necessity of raising water rates, and the possibility of being caught in a legal violation of the bond ordinance.

While the city might have managed to quiet the first two public manifestations of fiscal stress, the third event was unavoidably conspicuous. The city was going to market with a bond to build a shopping center on the edge of town to increase the tax base. However, the bond issue was given a low rating of BAA which was not only publicly embarrassing but also expensive because it required additional interest. Just at this time New York City was tottering on the brink of bankruptcy, and Southside's city council became genuinely frightened at the possibility of a similar misfortune. Much of the effort exerted to improve the city's finances over the next few years explicitly aimed at improving the bond rating. Two years later city officials were disturbed to realize that these efforts had barely maintained the rating. Worse still, they faced the serious danger of an even lower rating or perhaps none at all, in which case they could not enter the money market.

The city was seriously embarrassed by all three events. A former budget officer was recalled to help handle the problems. He made a presentation to the council regarding the extent and location of deficits, the degree of underfunding, and the structure of the budget. Real budget cutbacks followed. A number of positions were eliminated, eighteen in the Police Department alone. Of the eighteen, eight cuts were due to attrition. To replace them six people were hired with CETA funds. The Fire Department also lost four slots and the Street Department seven. The net reduction for the whole city, which represented about 2.5% of the total full time equivalent personnel was thirteen positions, including those on grants. The Police Department, which took the brunt of the cuts, underwent considerable reorganization. The Officer Friendly program was eliminated, patrol zones were consolidated, and the Youth Division was merged with Investigations. The Street Department reduced catch basin cleaning and cut street sweeping in half. Fire Department captains took the jobs of retiring assistant chiefs.

Aside from personnel cuts, there was reallocation of revenue sharing money, which formerly had been given partly to Civil Defense/ Public Safety and partly to community social service agencies. After the budget cuts, the entire amount went to the Police and Fire Departments. The Community Relations Department was also cut back.

In addition to the budget cuts, there was some attempt to improve the structure of the budget and budgetary control. The budget was somewhat simplified so that the council could understand it better. It was fully computerized so that individual department's expenditures could be tracked month by month, a task formerly completed by hand a couple of times a year. The city manager attempted to introduce program budgeting, but the department heads did not like it and it lasted only one year. The budget format included explicit references to expenses incurred in prior years. The Fire Department, which had been running a deficit, was taken out of the General Fund, and a new tax was levied to pay for it.

In the next two years the council and city administrators tried both to control expenditure and increase revenue. To achieve the former, they watched more closely the amount of overtime in departments and gave smaller raises to unionized employees. The council established a new personnel office to control patronage and establish personnel policies, and it demanded and received more detailed financial impact data on proposed annexations and other extensions of city services. It also considered a broader range of options for intergovernmental cooperation, especially with the township and the county. The city tried to reduce insurance costs by requiring defensive driving courses for all city personnel. The city manager tried to take control over costs of automobile maintenance but had not succeeded at the time when he was fired.

To increase revenues, the city increased property taxes. During the period of fiscal stress, property tax rates tripled. The council also tried to increase revenues by rebuilding portions of the downtown. The council also decided to put more effort into getting government grants and therefore hired a grantsman.

After a year of no salary increases at all, layoffs and small salary increases brought union trouble. There was a week-long strike in 1977. The city manager was fired because of a combination of mismanagement of the deficits, labor troubles, and his handling of the downtown redevelopment project—all related to financial problems. An older man experienced with both budgets and budget cutting was hired in his place. Within a year the new city manager had eliminated the last deficits ahead of schedule. Yet the financial problems of the city were not over, and many of the underlying problems which generated fiscal stress were still unresolved.

Budget Analysis

From the point of view of budget analysis, what happened to the city to get into such a terrible bind? Was there a revenue shortfall? Were revenues overestimated? Did expenditures grow too rapidly?

One of the first questions about the history of city revenues is whether revenues suddenly dropped below expectations for reasons beyond the city's immediate control, and whether such a drop caused deficits in various funds.[2] Analysis of the budget data suggests that in one case the city overestimated grant revenues, probably because of inadequate experience in dealing with the federal government. Aside from this particular overestimation of revenue, revenue was rather closely estimated. An example of estimated and actual revenue for sales taxes is shown in table 2.1.

Table 2.1
Estimated and Actual Sales Tax Revenue

1969 actual	$1,636,005
1970 estimate	1,999,023
1970 revised estimate[a]	2,223,289
1971 initial estimate	2,433,689
1971 actual	2,488,056
1972 estimate	2,787,571
1972 actual	2,734,165
1973 estimate	3,007,480
1973 actual	2,889,318
1974 estimate	3,033,783
1974 actual	2,967,666
1975 estimate	3,191,050
1975 actual	3,361,811
1976 estimated	3,371,610
1976 actual	3,846,131
1977 estimated	?
1977 actual	4,076,898

Source: Budget data
[a]Based on 6 mos. actual.

The city did experience additional shortfalls. In one case, the total assessed valuation began to fluctuate. This was partly the result of an apparent drop in total assessed valuation of real estate. In 1971, 1972, and 1973, there was no increase in assessed valuations, although an increase would have generated enough revenue to prevent deficits. The change in assessed valuation is shown in table 2.2. The increase in assessed values after 1973 disguises the fact that from 1973 through the period of the field work the sales value of the downtown area declined each year.[3]

In addition to the overestimation of federal grant revenue and the stagnation of assessed valuations, the city had a third revenue prob-

Table 2.2
Extent of Financial Stress

Year	Deficits (in millions)	Assessed Valuation	Tax Rate Dollars (hundred assessed)
1971	.27	256,580,336	$1.1773
1972	.44	250,762,349	1.1825
1973	1.4	255,886,097	1.6009
1974	2.5	262,170,565	2.1994
1975	4.3[a]	264,747,138	2.5934
1976	3.8 (est)	279,925,202	3.1076 (est)[b]
1977	2.2 (est)	. . . .	3.8735 (est)[b]

Sources: Deficits are from a memo from the budget director to the mayor and council. Tax rates 1971–74 are from auditors' reports; the 1975 rate and 1976 and 1977 estimated rates are from a memo from the city manager to the mayor and council, August 24, 1977.
[a]The deficit is nearly 20% of the city's budget
[b]Tax rate estimates were based on assumptions of stable assessed valuation.

lem which resulted from the pattern of tax collection. The county collected all property taxes and then turned them over to the other governmental units. When the county began to experience financial difficulties, it kept the revenue instead of disbursing it, which forced the local governments to borrow until such time as the county released these funds.[4] A political squabble between township assessor and the county resulted in no property tax distribution for one entire year. This exaggerated the city's already serious cash flow problems and elevated costs even further because the city had to pay interest on warrants during the whole period. This exacerbated the city's own problem but did not cause the large deficits.

While the city's revenue problems did contribute to fiscal stress, it is not accurate to say that unexpected drops in revenue caused the deficits. The evidence against such a thesis is that the city budgeted deficits—planned them in advance—before actual revenues were known. In certain fund accounts the city planned to spend more than it expected to receive. The amounts of planned budgeted deficits are shown in table 2.3.

There is a sense in which the city's revenue did not grow fast enough to cover rising expenditures, but this alone is an insufficient explanation. No matter what the cause of fiscal stress, it is always true that there would not be any problem if only there were more money.

Table 2.3
Budgeted and Actual Deficits by Fund Account

	General[a] Corporate	Police[b]	Road and Bridges[b]
1972 budgeted deficit	$ 186,571	$ 321,666	$ 71,561
1972 actual	169,768	221,478	139,064
1973 budgeted deficit	270,064	319,968	146,376
1973 actual deficit	670,810	477,823	311,566
1974 budgeted deficit	1,601,344	1,782,130	844,210
1974 actual deficit	1,271,151	1,178,819	763,444
1975 budgeted deficit	1,743,804	2,576,772	1,139,887

Source: Memo to councilmen from Finance Director.
[a]Include Fire Department.
[b]Excludes pension funds.

Fiscal stress arises when appropriate steps are not taken to avoid deficits within a limited budget.

Before the general economic decline of the city can be blamed, the expenditure issue must be explored. If in fact expenditures were moderate and hiring was controlled, and normal salary increases were more than the growth in revenue could sustain, then one can conclude that slow growth of the tax base caused the fiscal stress. On the other hand, if expenditures increased rapidly due to union settlements, departmental expansion, or pressure groups, one may conclude that administrative problems and/or political vulnerability prevented the city from keeping expenditures within the bounds of revenue.

What does documentary analysis of expenditures suggest? Initially one must locate the deficits in the budget. The funds showing deficits were the Police Protection fund, the General Fund, and the Road and Bridges Fund. The budget itself did not show which department caused the deficits in the General Fund, but other sources clarified that it was the Fire Department. In the Roads and Bridges Fund, the key department was streets. The amounts of yearly deficits in each fund are shown in table 2.3.

There were a series of expenditure problems, especially noticeable in the Police Protection Fund, which had the largest deficits. Through the mid-sixties the Police Department had remained stable in size and had paid the officers low salaries as compared with private industry. The expansion of the police force began in the late 1960s at precisely the time in which tax rates were being reduced. Just when more taxes were needed to support a bigger, more professional police force, the council continued to vote for expansion without making the necessary financial adjustments. The history of the Police Deparment personnel growth and personnel-related costs is shown in table 2.4.

Table 2.4
Police Department Growth 1966–1976

	Personnel Services	Capital Outlay	Total Expenditures	Expenditures 1967 dollars[a]	Number of Sworn Officers
1966	$ 653,848	$ 4,091	$ 737,005	$ 756,679	81
1967	852,276	20,179	973,395	973,395	82
1968	1,036,803	8,468	1,173,730	1,125,340	93
1969	1,181,483	16,157	1,413,915	1,286,547	120[b]
1970	1,513,718	28,864	1,809,826	1,555,170	–
1971	1,698,959	101,155	2,078,864	1,720,914	–
1972	1,836,566	22,035	2,196,149	1,766,813	156
1973	2,009,958	69,935	2,526,546	1,914,050	168
1974	2,398,985	54,500	2,915,780	1,995,743	181
1975	3,206,934	99,503	3,897,743	2,473,187	205
1976	. . . .	. . . . . .	. . . .	. . . .	191

Sources: Police Department memo to city manager on columns 1–4. Number of sworn officers 1966–1969 is from a consultant's report. Number of officers 1972–1976 is from city personnel records.

[a]Calculated using a regional consumer price index.

[b]The increase in sworn officers was composed of 20 patrolmen and 7 sergeants.

It is impossible to document the growth of deficits in the Fire Department because until 1978 the Fire Department was part of the General Fund. Since all revenue was pooled in the General Fund, one cannot conclude that too little tax was raised for Fire Protection in particular. The chief of the Fire Department conceded, however, that the department had been running chronic deficits. He blamed them on union settlements. According to budget figures, his analysis was partly true. While the size of the department increased somewhat, its expansion was not comparable to that of the Police Department. The Police Department added fifty persons from 1972 to 1975, the years of growing deficits, while the Fire Department added fifteen men (twenty-four of the new policemen were added in 1975).

The smallest deficit was the Road and Bridges Fund, which, nevertheless, showed planned deficits of over a million dollars in 1975. From 1972 to 1975, the Street Department added twelve new people, of whom ten were hired in 1975. While the new employees' salaries alone could not account for the size of the Street Department deficits, such a large expansion on the heels of discovering the extent of deficits seems odd.

More detailed analysis of the departments running deficits is shown in table 2.5.

From these data it is clear that there was an expenditure problem in addition to the revenue problems noted above. The Fire Department averaged budget increases of 14% a year for the five years preceding fiscal stress, the Police averaged 18% a year in increases, and the Street Department grew by an average of 21% a year. Salary increments only partly explained these increases.[5] The city continued to add new employees and increased other parts of the budget as well.

The impact of labor costs on budgeted increases was greatest in the Police Department. This means that most of the growth in budgets was accounted for by increases in salary and the number of personnel. Sixty-four percent of the increases in regular wages from 1971 to 1975 were due to salary increments, while 36% of the increase in wages was due to personnel expansion. Salary increase and personnel expansion together accounted for 69% of the total budgeted increases in the department during the years of growing deficits. Salary hikes alone account for 44% of the average annual increase.

During the same years, 69% of the increase in Fire Department wages was due to salary increments. This reflected a somewhat slower hiring rate than that of the police, and slightly more generous salary increments. Thirty-one percent of the wage increase was for new personnel. The combination of salary increases and new personnel accounted for only 42% of the overall budget increase; salary increase alone accounted for only about 29% of the total increase.

In the Street Department, only 46% of the rise in wages was due to larger salaries, while 54% of the wage increase was for new personnel. Salary and personnel increase together equalled 43% of the total budget increase. Salary increase alone accounted for 13% of the average budget increase.

It is clear from these data that the departments had rather strikingly different patterns of expansion, although some overall generalizations

Table 2.5
Expenditure Increases In Three Departments
Running Deficits, 1971–1978

		% budget increase over prior year	% salary increase	Sal. incr. as % of increase in reg. wages	Wage increase[b] as % of total increase expenditures
1971	Fire	− 5.8	10.7	50	(undefined)[a]
	Police	14.8	10.2	100	51
	Streets	22.9	11.4	51	43
1972	Fire	20	5.5	46	47
	Police	12	5.5	70	50
	Streets	− 16	5.5	10	(undefined)[a]
1973	Fire	12	6.2	95	40
	Police	17	5.5	43	91
	Streets	18	4.0	49	51
1974	Fire	25	13.6	73	54
	Police	28	9.8	35	71
	Streets	12	8.2	100	25
1975	Fire	20	16.0	82	68
	Police	19	15.6	73	82
	Streets	68	5.8	14	32
1976	Fire	− 13	1.	100	(undefined)[a]
	Police	− 2	− 1.1	7% of decrease is salary decrement.	81% of decrease is wages.
	Streets	− 32	4.8	−	10% of decrease is wages.
1977	Fire	24	7.	75	31
	Police	17	7.	57	54
	Streets	18	7.	100	10
1978	Fire	10	1.6 + 6%	33	87
	Police	22	2.9 + 6%	37	77
	Streets	12	8.6 + 6%	100	20% of decrement is in wages.

[a]These values are given as undefined since wages did increase, but the total budget decreased. Wages, therefore, cannot account for an increase or a decrease in the budget.
[b]Wage increase is a combination of salary increments plus salary of new employees.

are possible. Clearly the budgets were not at a standstill. Routine salary increases did not account for the bulk of budgeted increases. Salary increases varied from 13% to 44% of total budgeted increases. Additions to personnel were also important in elevating costs. However, another element of cost increases made an impact. It consisted primarily of capital outlays and secondarily of contractual services. There were virtually no increases in the costs of commodities, in which one would expect to find inflationary impact. Capital expenditures were made for building new fire stations and purchasing new fire trucks, new squad cars for police, and motorized mobile equipment for the Streets Department. That these expenditures accounted for a substantial portion of the budget was a significant fact. How these items got into the budget and what they represented will be discussed in later chapters.

In summary, Southside had both a revenue and an expenditure problem. Total assessed valuation dropped, yielding less revenue than anticipated. City politicians and administrators continued to expend greater amounts in discretionary areas without increasing tax rates until the crisis was well-developed. The police, fire, and street departments were running deficits. The causes of the declining revenues and increased expenditures will be discussed in the next three chapters.

Three

Economic Base Erosion and Migrations: Causes of Fiscal Stress

The first group of causes of urban fiscal stress to be discussed here is the economic base/population migration argument. Proponents of this position argue that, regardless of political contributions to fiscal stress, economic base erosion, with its attendant population shifts, underlies the rest. In Southside, the erosion of the economic base was reflected in a leveling off and decline of total assessed valuation. Not only does this economic base erosion underlie the fiscal problems in a causal sense, but it also predates the political responses in a historical sense. Therefore, it is reasonable to analyze the economic base erosion/population migration argument first. In examining these underlying causes of fiscal stress, the city's growth and decline will be described in the broadest terms, and the impact of migrations will be explored independently.

Growth and Decline

Growth and decline are often cited as the causes of urban fiscal stress. Actually, they encompass a number of different variables and proposed mechanisms for generating fiscal stress. Growth and decline can be viewed in four ways, each independent but related to the others: industrial or business growth and decline (especially as measured by the number of jobs generated); population growth and decline; areal growth and stagnation; and physical growth and decay (especially as measured by new construction).[1]

In a simplified model of the relationships between these aspects of growth and decline, more businesses attract more people, and more people require more space, which encourages annexation and/or new construction.[2] Decline occurs when businesses are no longer competitive and either die or move out, creating a reduction in jobs, followed by population decline and lowered occupancy rates. Physical decay follows.[3] The fiscal impact of this pattern is loss of revenues on the one hand and inability to cut back costs to match the declining population on the other.

The simple model of growth and decline can be elaborated in a number of ways. With respect to growth, particular growth strategies become salient: is the city annexing new land, and, if so, at what capital and service costs and with what hope of return? If the city is growing denser, the degree of density, its location, and consequences for city services and for the potential of later retrenchment may be relevant. The population composition in terms of race, income, and skills may be relevant to city revenues and expenditures, to the unemployment rate, and to the level of political activism. The type of businesses attracted to the city, their match to the labor pool, and their ability to move to cheaper locations may also be relevant to patterns of growth and decline. With respect to decline in particular, people may or may not emigrate when business migrates, and people sometimes migrate for reasons not related to loss of jobs.

In short, analysis of growth and decline must focus not just on net population gains and losses, but on changing population composition, which affects both revenues and service demands, and on the size of and nature of the labor pool. The fiscal implications of growth must be emphasized as well as the implications of decline, since the effects of growth can lag into the period of decline, and patterns of city growth can affect both service requirements and the degree of cost rigidity when retrenchment occurs.

The patterns of growth and decline observed in Southside support the view that these long-term trends of growth and decline contributed to the fiscal crisis, but not inevitably nor exactly as suggested by the literature.

Industrial Growth and Decline

The city's industrial base has always been relatively undiversified. Through the early 1900s the city was an important railroad center, active particularly in the distribution of foods. In the early 1900s the city became important in the production of steel. By the 1960s, the steel industry had slackened somewhat, and petrochemicals became the city's dominant industry. In the late 1960s the federal government closed an arsenal facility outside the city limits. Four or five other companies left the city in the next few years, some for the suburbs, some for other parts of the country. In 1970 the census reported a population increase over 1960 and a continued low unemployment rate. Apparently the jobless migrated and were replaced by in-migrants who could find jobs.

The stagnation of business from 1968 onward had a direct impact on the fiscal crisis to the extent that it contributed to the stagnation of assessed valuation. But *loss* of business was not the direct cause of fiscal crisis, because the city annexed land for a shopping mall and managed to keep most of the businesses inside the city limits. However, businesses were retained at great expense. Annexation had not only a high cost but also the secondary impact of emptying out the downtown and threatening assessed valuations. The impact of business stagnation on the fiscal crisis was thus continuous, first as a precipitating event, and later as a cause of the prolongation of fiscal stress.

Population

The second aspect of growth and decline is population. The city's population grew relatively constantly until it dropped during the Great Depression, after which it regained momentum. From World War II to 1970, the population nearly doubled. In the mid-seventies, the rate of growth slowed and then reversed. The history of the city's population growth is detailed in table 3.1.

The slackening of population growth in the 1970s seems to have reflected the increase in the percentage of blacks and Hispanics, the enlargement of the black and Hispanic ghettos, and the out-migration of whites. The proportion of blacks and Hispanics grew rapidly. In 1960, 6.9% of the population were black; by 1970, 12% were black. As of 1977, city estimates were 18% black and 7% Hispanic. If the census figures for mid-decade population are correct, then there must have been some white outward migration.

The interpretation of population decline and its importance for fiscal stress is problematic. Population decline per se may not be harmful. If, for example, population decline follows a plant closing, it means that the jobless are leaving the city to find employment elsewhere. Such migration may actually be healthy, since there will be no accumulation of the poor to consume services for which they are unable to pay.[4] If, however, population decline results from an exodus of stable white middle-class families with an increasing concentration

Table 3.1
Land Area, Population, Population Change, and Density for Selected Years

Year	Area (sq. mi.)	Population	Percentage Pop. Increase & Decrease	Density (pop./sq. mi.)
1835[a]	.28	2,558	–	9135
1940	10.00	42,365	– 1.5[b]	4236
1950	10.00	51,601	21.8	5160
1960	11.50	66,780	29.4	5806
1970	16.50	78,804	20.4	4776
1971	20.25	81,800	1.8	4039
1972	20.40	82,800	1.2	4058
1975	23.03	85,700	3.2	3721
1978[a]	22.94[c]	80,276	– 6.3	3499

Source: Planning Department.
[a] Area and Population statistics were taken from the 1978 budget.
[b] This drop is with respect to 1930 population.
[c] Area probably did not decline; a parcel believed to be annexed may not have actually been annexed.

of poor blacks under ghetto conditions, there may indeed be serious fiscal implications. The service needs of the poor are great, yet the tax base is diminished.

In Southside the linkage between population decline and stress was not primarily the result of increased services to the poor. The increase in ghetto development did generate more calls to the Fire and Police departments,[5] but these did not bring about major new or increased services to the ghetto such as greater intensity of patrols.[6] Ghetto enlargement did not produce fiscal stress through direct service costs so much as through *increased fear of crime outside the ghetto*. Fear of crime increased demand for police from residents *outside* the ghetto and accelerated white flight to the suburbs. The flight to the suburbs generated a wave of annexations which cost the city a lot of money.

Areal Growth

The city had experienced rapid population growth from the end of World War II until 1970, and yet from 1945 until 1960 the area of the city remained almost constant. Many of the new residents moved directly inside the city's boundaries, which increased the city's density. Between 1960 and 1970, the number of blacks coming to the city grew. Almost half of the population growth between 1960 and 1970 was black. The blacks settled primarily on the city's east side. During the same decade, for the first time, whites began to settle outside the city limits. Some of these whites were probably newcomers; others, however, were old-timers moving out of the east side. The city annexed these new white settlements, almost doubling its area from 1960 to 1971. This growth continued into the 1970s. After the fiscal crisis began, the city leaders decided that annexation of residential land was too expensive in terms of services required and revenues generated. They changed to a policy of annexing only land with business on it or land suitable for businesses. Annexation continued, however, right through 1975, the year of the greatest deficits.

The annexations of the 1960s and early 1970s were haphazard. They consisted primarily of single family homes or vacant lots. Several informants stated that the city had laid water mains going nowhere. These unselective annexations turned out to be bad investments. In the mid-1970s the city annexed a large plot of land for the proposed shopping center. The initial costs for this annexation were high and initial returns low. For a summary of the city's history of areal growth see table 3.1.

Geographic expansion continued during the 1960s and 1970s. Not only did this annexation require intensive capital investment, but it also required increasing service.[7] For example, the deficits in the Fire Department can be explained by the expanded area. In 1969 a consultant's report on the Fire Department argued that to improve its fire rating the city would have to build new fire stations in the new parts of the city, buy equipment for the fire stations, and hire additional firemen. Much of the Fire Department's expansion was to comply with this report. Fire Department expansion continued through the 1970s, when the Fire Department decided to build a new station on the site of the newly annexed shopping mall. Thus it was not the demands or needs of the deteriorating downtown which generated deficits in the Fire Protection Fund so much as the physical expansion of the city, which was partly due to the effort to recapture the out-migrating whites.

The expansion of several other city departments was also directly related to areal expansion. For example, a new sewage treatment plant had to be built on the west side in 1972 to accommodate growth, and new staff had to be hired to run it. This expansion fed into the fiscal problems when the Water and Sewer Fund nearly defaulted in 1975. The expansion of the Street Department, along with the acquisition of new equipment, was directly related to the annexation of the shopping center. While residential annexation frequently left paving to builders, the city's arrangement with the developer left the burden of streets on the city.

Areal growth was thus a direct cause of increased costs. While it does not explain all the cost increases in the deficit funds, it accounts for nearly all the expansion in the Fire Department and much of the expansion in the Street Department. Areal expansion was also related to increased costs for sewer and water, although the Water and Sewer Department contributed less directly to the deficits because it was financed by bonds. That these costs rose without a commensurate increase in revenues greatly contributed to the financial crisis. In part, the inability of revenues to keep up with costs resulted from the nature of annexations, with their heavy up-front costs. But also it was related to the choice of land for annexation, some areas of which would never generate as much in revenues as they would cost in services. Part of the revenue-expenditure gap also derived from the fact that the purpose of annexations was more to recapture escaping population than to accommodate new arrivals.[8] There was no new population to build and buy or to pay property, sales, and income taxes. The city was running in place—expanding its area to maintain rather than to increase the level of taxes.

This analysis suggests a combination of two recognized themes not joined in any one familiar model. The first is that suburbanization, the exodus of the middle classes, and increasing concentration of the poor in the central cities generates expenses and little revenue. The second theme is that, without sustained economic growth, continuous annexation of land becomes a financial burden. What happened in Southside was an exodus of whites to unincorporated areas, annexation of which required extensive investments in capital and services despite the fact that real growth in economy and population had stopped. The annexation of new retail development followed much the same pattern of recapturing fleeing businesses rather than increasing the number of businesses inside the city limits. Much of the growth in expenditures during the fiscal crisis was a delayed effect of annexing large amounts of land rather than an effect of increased service to the poor. Areal expansion is likely to contribute to fiscal stress because it is not reversible when revenues decline and because it involves heavy up-front costs to be made up later. Expansion, therefore, is very sensitive to fluctuations in current revenue because it sometimes does not generate revenue to cover outgo for several years.

After emphasizing the importance of annexation, it is necessary to add a few warnings. First, because the effects of areal growth may hold over into periods of population decline, the effects of the one may easily be mistaken for the effects of the other. Secondly, many factors influence whether or not the city's area grows. Sometimes a city is hemmed in by other cities and towns and cannot expand; sometimes annexation is forced on a city by its own ordinances (for example, if a neighborhood votes to become part of the city, the city may not refuse it). But for the most part, annexation is a political decision (laced with economic considerations). Thirdly, large annexations do not have automatic impacts on the budget. Annexation agreements are negotiated with the city and specify the city's investment, and increases in staffing and service levels are mediated by departments and council members. It is possible to provide only a few new services and allow existing service levels to be watered down.

Physical Growth and Decline

Yet another type of growth and decline occurs in the physical plant of the city. Physical decline directly affects the assessed valuation and the attractiveness of an area, which in turn affect the desirability of living in the city. The city's overall pattern of physical growth began on the west bank of a river running north and south through what is now the old city. Settlement gradually expanded eastward across the river to the area which became downtown. Much of the housing in this area dates from the 1880s. The newer suburban growth took place almost completely on the west side. Since most of the west side is newer, its streets, water mains, lights, and the like are in much better condition than those on the east side.

The new migrants, the blacks and Hispanics, settled on the aging east side in the oldest and poorest neighborhoods surrounding the downtown central business district. Through a combination of processes involving absentee landlords, poor maintenance, prejudice, and disinvestment, these neighborhoods became an expanding slum. Compared with averages for the whole city, twice as many fires occurred in these neighborhoods, probably because of the age of the housing, building code violations, and arson. The result was numerous burned out, empty homes that undermined confidence in the entire neighborhood and retarded reinvestment.

Physical deterioration of the aging east side was partly the result of expanding black and Hispanic slums and partly the result of a lack of city investment. Capital projects were delayed or ignored. The water system had been allowed to deteriorate to the point that it no longer functioned. Sewage treatment was minimum. Untreated sewage flowed into streams and across people's yards. Sewage back-ups were frequent. There was no separate storm drainage system, and floods were frequent. Roads were in terrible disrepair. The city's fire rating dropped, partly because of low water pressure. There were no street lights in some of the neighborhoods. The city did not invest in capital needs anywhere in the city, but this neglect was most obvious on the old east side.

Along with the surrounding neighborhoods, the downtown was also physically decaying. The deterioration of the old downtown was an integral part of the fiscal crisis, because the total assessed valuation of the downtown began to decline. The physical deterioration was the result of both social change and political decisions concerning expenditures.

Migrations and Social Change

The social fabric of a city can affect its finances in many ways. For example, if political lines of cleavage follow economic lines, the city may be characterized by "class politics." The poor may be organized to make expensive demands on the city while property owners press for tax relief.[9] Another line of cleavage may develop out of the antagonism between ethnic groups. High degrees of animosity may lead to highly segregated neighborhoods, quick turnover when a disliked ethnic groups moves in, and accelerated disinvestment.[10] Such animosity may also generate a high level of ghetto development, crime, and fear, which leads to added police expenditures.[11]

In Southside, white ethnic groups settled in the city to work in the steel mills. They lived, and continue to live, in segregated neighborhoods, each retaining some of its ethnic character. When blacks began to move into the city, they were unable to get well-paying jobs. The steel mills were not hiring, and blacks tended to have insufficient education for jobs in the petrochemical industry.[12] Blacks did find jobs, but mostly in lower-paying areas. Their lower median family income is apparent in table 3.2.

The blacks and later the Hispanics settled on the east side near the downtown. Their homes frequently lacked water hookups, and some areas had no paved roads. There were few lights in the residential and downtown areas. Roads were rutted and in bad condition. Sewage and

Table 3.2
Comparative Family Income, Blacks and All Families

	Median Family Income—All	Median Family Income—Blacks
1960	$ 6,958	$4,351
1970	11,900	8,700

Source: U.S. Census of Population, 1960, 1970.

water, a problem throughout the city, plagued the area with floods and sewer backups. There were few parks. Relations between the blacks and police were poor and yet seemed to be their major contact with the city government. Blacks, surveyed by the Office of Community Relations in 1972, did not seem to know how to complain to city hall. Few citizens in these neighborhoods were registered to vote, and only a small percentage of those registered actually voted.

By 1966, the blacks began to demonstrate in the downtown area and make demands on the city. Their style was confrontational. The city manager at the time wrote a memo to the mayor informing him of the planned demonstrations and the hostility they would arouse, both of which would increase the difficulty of making the important social changes required.

About the same time some of the exclusively white west side schools acquired their first black students, and rioting broke out. The schools had to be closed. The mayor set up a citizens' committee to look into the disturbances, and had a human relations expert from Washington, D.C., advise the group. What they came up with eventually was a new city Department of Community Relations to handle relations with the blacks. It replaced an earlier Office of Human Relations and increased its budget from ten thousand dollars to forty thousand dollars per year. Its function was to help alleviate job discrimination and, later, housing discrimination, but it was never given the authority or budget to do a proper job.[13]

At the time of Martin Luther King's assassination, portions of the black neighborhoods went up in flames. Buildings were set afire, and firemen battling the fires were stoned. Buildings were looted, and windows smashed in the downtown area. A curfew was imposed and businesses were closed for five days. When it became clear the city could not handle the rioting, state troopers and the National Guard were summoned. Whites watched the burning buildings in fear, and many reportedly armed themselves. To contain any spillover and prevent vigilantism, the bridges across the river were pulled up. Whatever prejudice the whites had felt earlier was crystallized and seemingly justified by the riots.

After the riots were over, a delegation of blacks presented the city with a list of the riot's causes:

1. Lack of job opportunities
2. Police harassment
3. Improper use of federal funds in the public schools
4. Inadequate housing and the need for an open housing law
5. Failure to teach Negro-related subjects such as Negro history in the schools
6. Lack of progress on sewer and water
7. Lack of small business opportunities
8. Inadequate recreational facilities
9. Lack of courtesy to blacks in downtown business establishments
10. The need to close an open cesspool in one of the black neighborhoods

The city, in cooperation with other agencies and special districts, tried to handle a number of these issues. With the help of the Chamber of Commerce, local jobs were found and a summer job program for black teenagers was started. The Police Department changed its recruiting practices to eliminate violence-prone and emotionally disturbed applicants. The city passed an open housing ordinance in 1969. The Park District built a park in the northeastern area of black neighborhoods. The Water and Sewer Department eliminated the open cesspool and continued to try to improve the old and ailing water system. Low income housing was built by HUD and private capital.

The cost to the city of satisfying the demands of the poor was minimal. Much of what these representatives of the poor blacks asked for was beyond the city's scope. The city could not provide housing. It could not alter the expenditure of school funds or the existing curriculum. It could not assure that blacks would be treated courteously in downtown stores. Passing an open housing ordinance did not cost the city any money, and closing the open sewer was a small project. The only additional direct cost was the expansion of the Human Relations Department, at an additional cost of thirty thousand dollars. The city did not allocate much money to satisfy blacks' demands. However, the antagonism which was roused and simultaneously justified among the city's white citizens was a condition which would cost the city more in police protection than all the programs for the poor.[14]

The history of Police Department expansion suggests that the riots after Martin Luther King's assassination were an important stimulant to growth in expenditures. The number of police officers had remained unchanged for many years despite a consultant's report in the middle sixties suggesting the department was understaffed. After the riots, the recommendations were suddenly implemented, and there was a large increase in the number of new hires. New equipment was purchased and communications were improved, much of the expense funded by grants. Equally important, the policemen and firemen who were involved in riot control and firefighting during the disturbance were the object of intense hatred by local citizens. This dangerous work helped build strong ties among police and firemen. All these factors—loss of esteem, danger, and unity—contributed to strengthening the unions. In 1969 the unions presented the council with a demand for a contract. Popular sentiment in the white community favored the action because the city's uniformed employees had protected them during the riots.

To summarize the impact of social change on the financial situation, the migrations of poor blacks to the city set in motion an important aspect of the city's problem. Blacks did not respond to poor conditions through an organized voting bloc nor by neighborhood associations, but abruptly, as demonstrators in the streets. Their demands were heard and the city made an attempt to comply with them, but at minimal dollar cost. The real impact of the black (and later Hispanic) ghettos was threefold: (1) they hastened the exodus of whites and set in motion the annexations mentioned above; (2) they hastened the decline of property values in the downtown, which they surrounded; and (3) they increased white demand for police to provide protection for downtown store owners and citizens in general. The mediating mechanism for much of what occurred was racism and discrimination.

To conclude the chapter, the portrait of growth and decline and population migrations offered in this chapter suggests an alternative to a familiar model of decline:

1. The chapter argues that increased annexation (growth) following population exodus (suburbanization) resulting in part from ghettoization of black migrants contributed to *increasing costs*, especially in the Fire Department. While looking for causes of declining revenue, we found instead one major source of (lagged) expenditure increases,

and a partial answer to why the number of employees and the size of budgets continued to increase even though revenue stabilized.

2. The chapter argues that viewing the migrations as shifts in the proportion of revenue producers and revenue consumers is not only too simple, but it may also in some situations be incorrect. Increasing service costs may accompany increased ghettoization without any increased services to the poor (from local revenues). In Southside, the increased costs of the Fire Department were primarily the result of extension of services to the newly annexed white suburbs. The demands put by black community members were mostly beyond the city's capacity to provide. Polarization of the races, combined with grant income, contributed to expansion of police personnel. The experience of the riots made heroes of uniformed employees and contributed to the strength of the unions. All these factors heightened costs. The model discussed in Chapter 1 underestimates the fiscal impact of social cleavages created by migrations and the direct impact of one migration on another, not mediated by tax increases caused by social services to the poor. And the model overestimates, at least for this round of fiscal stress, the impact of net loss of jobs.

3. Finally, the chapter argues that the economic base erosion/population migration model underestimates the importance of government and politics. The narrow scope of government was important in determining the fiscal impact of the migrations. The increase in police after the riots was a political response. The annexations and negotiations surrounding them were political decisions and staff functions. The underinvestment in capital projects that contributed to physical decay was a political outcome. The chapter suggests that economic base erosion and population migrations may be only part of a larger process leading to fiscal stress.

Four

Political Process and Fiscal Stress: Structural Weaknesses

City policies of underinvestment in capital facilities contributed to physical decline. City policies of annexation shaped patterns of both area and service growth and made cutback difficult. City responses to ghetto development resulted in an expanded police force. But to understand the generation of deficits in Southside, one must understand why the political/administrative system framed the problems as it did, and why it translated them into deficits.

The literature on reformed government postulates that city manager government is less vulnerable to demands and therefore less likely to run into fiscal stress. With its antipatronage, professional orientation, city manager government should be lean and well-run. In theory, it should not run into the kinds of problems described in chapter 2. It is of considerable interest, therefore, that Southside did run into trouble. Was there something about the city manager form itself that contributed to fiscal stress?

In the ideal form of city manager government, the city manager is the chief executive, while the mayor is usually a ceremonial leader with little more power than an ordinary councilman. The council's purpose is to reflect public needs and desires and provide policy guidance, whereas the city manager and his staff, on the basis of technical expertise, carry out the will of the council. The city manager should maintain a low public profile and stay out of the newspapers and away from public conflicts. He has an impact on policy because he initiates ideas and recommendations to the council and can persistently remind political leaders of budgetary limitations.

The city manager form was designed to destroy city political machines and bossism. Consequently, it is supposed to eliminate patronage and reduce the influence of narrow interest groups, giving political control back to the people. At-large elections in small cities are supposed to reduce log-rolling, or pork barrel politics. Nonpartisan elections are supposed to divorce national and local politics, and prevent coattail elections and patronage appointments. The system is designed to eliminate the politics of bargaining between structurally opposed interest groups. In this sense, it is supposed to eliminate politics, endless debates and compromises and to reduce conflicts of all kinds.

With respect to finance, the designers of the city manager government made no elaborate claims of cheapness, only of efficiency. A system of control was made possible through the separation of politics and budgeting. Whereas in a strong mayor system, the chief executive is simultaneously responsible for satisfying political claims and maintaining a balanced budget (an unstable combination), in city manager government the mayor and council are responsible for satisfying political needs, while the city manager is responsible for a balanced budget. The city manager is supposed to act as a budget cutter, curtailing the requests of the departments. The council has final approval of the budget, but normally accepts the city manager's recommendation. In its ideal form, the city manager government should be less susceptible to deficits than the strong-mayor type.[1]

Southside's Departures from the Model

In a general way, the major political actors in Southside followed the roles outlined by the city manager form. The mayor was a "weak" mayor, with little more power than the councilmen. The city manager and staff were trained professionals. Elections were really nonpartisan, and the city had gone a long way toward the elimination of patronage appointments. Council meetings were the crucial decision-making stage, as they were supposed to be. Individual petitioners had easy access to the council, and much of the political process revolved around the attempt to satisfy petitioners in a reasonable way without permanently damaging the community as a whole. However, despite the overall conformity to city manager government there were a number of ways in which the ideals were never achieved. Possibly they never could have been achieved. The roles of policy formation and policy execution were muddled, the city manager was not always strong enough to curtail patronage, and interest groups did play a role in city politics.

The Roles of Policy Formation and Policy Execution

First, as many authors have noted, the distinction between policy formation and execution of decisions is a difficult one to make.[2] Not only is it difficult to separate decisions into neat policy and practice components, but even when possible, actors may prefer not to carry out the roles associated with the city manager format. In Southside, council members tried to avoid policy decisions as well as any other decisions which would divide their electorates. For example, the council gave the city manager little guidance on how to carry out labor negotiations (although some claimed they gave him advice which he ignored). The mayor's solution to the absence of a personnel policy was, rather than have the council responsible for policy, to set up a staff position to handle it.

While the city council frequently abdicated the policy role, the city staff took more decision-making control than specified by the ideal type. City staff set priorities among projects approved in the budget, bringing some to fruition and leaving others behind. The priorities were based on technical criteria, such as the size of the projects, workloads, materials on hand, and availability of grant funding. Within the area of grant-funded projects, city staff arranged projects in terms of expiration dates of funding, proportion of the project already completed, and the like. By the time staff was finished, there was little room for council discretion in setting priorities. In addition to setting priorities, the city manager also influenced the initiation of projects, techniques for achieving them, and their design and cost. The city manager did more than carry out the will of the majority of the council.

Because of the city manager's key role in bringing projects to fruition he often got involved in politics. In a battle over the construction of parking decks, he espoused one out of several possible strategies and became deeply enmeshed in the ensuing controversy. The minority faction, which opposed the project, blamed him for bringing the project to its successful conclusion. No one could separate the execution of a project from its support, so the city manager became identified with the dominant council faction. The split in the council made whatever he did seem offensive to the minority faction. The manager was so disliked by the minority faction that controversy mounted over abolishing the city manager form itself.

Similar role shifts have been widely observed in other manager-administered cities. Less often pointed out is the possible financial impact of such departures from the "ideal." The absence of council policy regarding personnel meant, in effect, that it could shift the blame for unpopular personnel decisions onto the city manager, which caused a gradual deterioration in relations between him and the city's employees. As head of the city's negotiating team the manager became less and less effective. He was viewed by union negotiators as an enemy and was not trusted. Since the council had no policy, it did not necessarily accept positions struck in bargaining. No one appeared to have the authority to negotiate. City staff did not come up with a consistent personnel policy, and perhaps could not without guidance from the council. The result was a confused muddle at negotiating time.

The politicization of the city manager role inevitably lessened his support from councilmembers who disagreed with his stance. Because the city council was empowered to hire and fire the city manager, its lack of support weakened his ability to curtail any budget requests from the council. The city manager feared for his job because of this structurally and historically weak position and because of the alienation of some of the council members when he tried to curtail their requests. The manager's weakness helped shape the budgetary process.

Not only did city staff end up playing more of a policy role than in the ideal type city manager government, but they also had less technical expertise than required to carry out policy. In fact, the problem of insufficient expertise to accomplish the job contributed to financial stress. The resources of the city manager's office were extremely limited. Various kinds of centralization for efficiency and control were impossible due to lack of staff, and when the fiscal crisis began, there was a serious shortage of experience and expertise in the budget office. The city staff also lacked experience in collective bargaining. In 1972 an experienced budget officer resigned. A new city manager hired a new young finance director, and it was the first budget for either of them. Inexperience led them to make a number of mistakes. Two years later, a second finance director, who turned out to be incompetent, was fired. At this point, a new assistant city manager took over budget preparation. The extent of deficits and the way in which they had been hidden finally came to light.

In labor negotiations, the city manager made a series of errors, some of which were costly, and he was ousted from the city's negotiating team. The assistant city manager, with no prior experience, took over.

He had neither authority to negotiate nor the skills to do so. Union officials felt that the city manager was still influencing negotiations despite his absence. These officials would not accept even very agreeable offers from the assistant city manager because they did not think he could make the council accept them. Effective city manager government depends on hiring knowledgeable and experienced managers. In this case, it appeared the job was changing too rapidly and was too difficult for some of the key personnel, especially in the areas of finance and labor relations.

Patronage: The Ideal and the Actual

One of the most important goals of city manager government is to control patronage. This is to be achieved in part by divorcing city politics from those of the national party. It is also to be achieved by personnel policies. Finally, it is to be achieved through the professional training of city managers, who take an oath to fight patronage and special interest government.

The absence of a party to hand out patronage positions to loyal campaigners was, in fact, achieved. In that sense there was no machine. However, the city did not really reform its personnel policies. There was no civil service system and virtually no personnel policy. Personnel problems had low priority for city staff. Because of the absence of civil service, the responsibility for curtailing patronage fell almost completely upon the city manager. The split council and his role in politics limited his ability to carry out this antipatronage mission.

Although there was no civil service, a board similar to a civil service board was in charge of police and fire personnel.[3] It was appointed by the mayor. City employees reported that although patronage appointments had ceased, promotions, handled by the politically appointed Police and Fire Board, were still given on the basis of favoritism. The results of examinations for promotion were handled peculiarly by the Police and Fire Board. For example, the Board waited for long periods of time to announce results, leading to charges of rigging test scores.

For the remaining city employees, there was virtually no personnel policy. As the assistant city manager explained:

> We have no organized personnel function. Because of our personnel policies and procedures, we turn over people faster. Peo-

ple become dissatisfied. It contributes to deficits because negotiators, including myself, have a competitive disadvantage. We don't
have the information we need to negotiate. Not all my time can be
devoted to personnel. I don't know all the grievances. . . . Grievances have gone to arbitration that a set of good personnel policies could have taken care of. There is no personnel policy. Each
department runs its own show.

. Because of a lack of detailed civil service rules and almost total
absence of personnel policies, much of the burden for controlling
patronage of all sorts fell on the city manager. During the 1950s and
1960s, the city manager had been no more than a city administrator,
with no power to curtail patronage appointments. By the time deficit
spending began in the early 1970s, a new city manager had taken over
who tried to curb patronage appointments, especially cases in which
councilmen insisted he find someone a job.

That same city manager retained his position throughout most of
the fiscal crisis. When he was interviewed in 1976 he was asked about
the number of patronage jobs. He said there were none.

. If a councilman calls and says, give so and so a job, that is the
kiss of death. The guy will go to the bottom of the list. The
furthest I will go is to say to the councilman, "If you think this
guy is good, I can guarantee he will get an interview." But if the
guy doesn't look good at the interview, that's it for him.

His concern, also expressed by the personnel director, seemed to be
that incompetent candidates would be forced onto the city staff. His
anger was directed less at political appointments or recommendations
per se than at unqualified candidates.[4]

The city manager's refusal to help sponsored candidates get jobs
made enemies for him on the council. Later, after he had been fired,
he brooded, analyzing the motives of each one who had voted against
him. He felt he had alienated one councilman in particular whose
nephew he had refused to hire, although the nephew had a police
record and was clearly unqualified. In addition to alienating councilmen by refusing to make patronage appointments, he alienated them
by cutting their pet projects in order to reduce deficits. He reflected, "I
don't think they ever forgave me."

As the years went by, the city manager's support on the council had
eroded, and he had begun to fear for his job.[5] Progressively he had lost

what control he had over patronage. A close friend of the city manager, when asked whether the manager had kept a tight rein on patronage, responded, "Not the last year or so. He was too worried about his job to control anything." Patronage hiring was not unbridled during that year but there was a noticeable loosening of strictures.

The financial impact of patronage at city hall is difficult to assess. The years of the greatest number of patronage appointments were years of presumed fiscal health, although this impression may be an artifact of inaccurate records during the machine era. During the years of the political machine, people were hired for political reasons, but on a per capita basis the city was not heavily overstaffed. By the early 1970s the government really had been reformed, and patronage hiring had been reduced. Not until close to the end of the fiscal crisis did the manager lose control over patronage, and even then there was no major increase in patronage hiring. It is unlikely, therefore, that *patronage* hiring was the cause of fiscal stress.

In short, the city manager was oriented against patronage in fact as well as in theory, especially where it would lead to ineffective employees. Toward the end of his administration, however, he began to lose control over patronage. Nevertheless, patronage did not seem to be the major cause of deficits. During the strong-mayor days, although appointments were political, the size of the city employment roles was limited. Later, the amount of political hiring was severely curtailed, although the number of employees increased. For a comparison between the number of city personnel in 1960 and 1975, see table 4.1.

Table 4.1
Employees per Thousand Population for Selected Years

Year	Population	Employees	Employees/Thousand Pop.
1960	66,780[a]	351[a]	5
1965	72,712[a]	329[a]	4
1970	78,644[a]	443[a]	5
1972	82,800[d]	537[b]	6
1975	76,500[c]	618[b]	8
1975	85,700[d]	—	7

[a]Census figures.
[b]Personnel files.
[c]Census estimate, special census.
[d]City planning department estimate.

Interest Groups: Ideal and Actual Roles

The prototype of city manager government would abolish interest group politics in favor of individual petitioners. Yet, in fact, interest groups were active at city hall. They were few, not representing every group or interest, and their competition with each other did not approximate an aggregative political process. In fact, they seldom competed or compromised with each other at all. In this sense, reality was close to the ideal. On the other hand, of the few interest groups present, some had close relations with both councilmen and city staff. This connection was contrary to the prototype because it suggested manipulation and hinted at politics in the negative sense, implying a political system closed to individual action.

The city manager characterized the politics of the city as dominated not by party but by special interests. Discussing some of the city's unwise annexations, in which water pipes were laid for the benefit of a single company, he offered "special interests" as the reason. According to one of the union leaders, "No one runs this city anymore (like the bosses used to)—now it's just the interest groups. Most of the council represents special interests. . . ."

With the possible exception of the city's unions, the existence and activity of the city's interest groups did not seem to be a major cause of fiscal stress. Some of the interest groups had an exceedingly narrow power base, or no power at all. The historical preservationists represented a very small number of voters: their major resource was tenacity (they almost wore the council down through sheer boredom). They did not succeed in accomplishing any of their goals during the study. The organized poor had no voting base, for their followers were often unregistered and even when registered often did not vote. Moreover, their activity as an interest group was sporadic. From 1966 to 1968, they did maintain a presence, if a confrontational stance can be described as a lobbying effort. During that period the city did not spend many dollars in responding to the blacks' demands. The downtown businessmen also had a narrow power base, since they could not deliver a large block of votes. The only power they had over the city was a vague threat to leave it. In many cases, the cost of moving was too great to make the threat credible. The downtown businessmen wanted increased police protection, better lighting, more parking, and a downtown mall. The cost to the city of satisfying the downtown businessmen, while large, was not paid out of current revenues, and was incurred in 1977, well after the deficits began. The businessmen paid for substantial portions of the downtown redevelopment and extra services out of special assessments. The businessmen did not have their own council member, only a lobbyist. The most they could do was suggest and persuade.

The unions and the banks were different, however, because they had some real power over the city. The banks purchased all the city's warrants and bonds. The city could not, or did not want to, go to tax anticipation *notes* despite their wider market. The notes would have to be rated, and therefore might publicly reveal continuing financial problems. The city was, therefore, quite dependent on the local banks. In turn, the banks held mortgages on many downtown properties. The decline in sales value threatened the banks and gave them an active interest in maintaining the downtown. The banks did have a representative on the council who actively supported downtown development. The downtown redevelopment project, however, did not begin until 1977 and so could not have caused the financial crisis.

The city employee unions exerted power not over the city collectively but over individual councilmen. In 1976 they elected two councilmen and almost unseated a third who was unsympathetic to them. From 1969 to 1972 or 1973, the unions had exerted power through popular sentiment, winning favorable contracts, generous benefits, and increased salaries. After that, they exercised power more as a result of internal solidarity in bargaining and interunion solidarity in maintaining effective strikes. The council did nothing to stop the unions because it feared the impact at the polls.

The organizational ambiguity of the city government—neither totally reformed nor totally unreformed—helped make the councilmen more dependent on the unions. No party machine or label guaranteed a broad base of support, and patronage with which to build a personal following was minimal. Yet the council was not so reformed that individual councilmen had no interest in political careers. By and large, they were interested in reelection, despite minimal resources and few organized voting constituencies. Consequently, they became dependent on the unions, and favorable action on union demands became the political currency with which to build a narrow coalition of voters. Fear of antagonizing unions prevented council members from formulating personnel policy. Lack of civil service and limited staff in the area of personnel, resulting in clumsy and expensive negotiations, further exacerbated the situation.

Southside never achieved the idealized version of city manager government. Like many other cities, the council determined policy less, and the city manager more, than in the prototype. The council's indecisiveness was felt most keenly in the area of personnel policy. It was magnified by the inexperience of the city manager and his assistant at negotiations. The split council and the political role of the city manager kept the latter's margin of support low and consequently weakened his ability to control costs and patronage (though patronage was probably not too much of a fiscal burden). The actual political structure also departed from the ideal in having active interest groups. However, these were few and, with the exception of the unions, probably did not contribute substantially to the generation of fiscal stress.

Political and Professional Goals

Ironically, the one way in which the city actually achieved the ideal contributed substantially to fiscal stress. Many of the city's staff positions were filled by people who had professional training and goals. These goals clashed with the goals of the politicians. Such a clash was not necessarily bad, since it could lead to a set of checks and balances. However, in Southside, the checks and balances broke down, with serious financial consequences.

The city staff's professionalism gave them a set of attitudes and goals beyond the skills required to do their jobs. These included decided visions of a good water system and how to attain it, a good fire or police department, and certain measurements of success. Professional staff often adopted the goal of quality rather than efficiency. They wanted the best equipment available rather than the cheapest that appeared to do the job. The time horizons of city staff and politicians were radically different. City staff were concerned with events twenty or thirty or more years later, while politicians generally seemed more concerned with the present. Clashes between professionals and politicians had been built into the city manager form of government; however, the idealized notion of the benefits derived from professional expertise ignored both the independence of professional goals and the inherent clash between political responsiveness and expert opinion.

A balance between political goals and professional goals will check the excesses of both. The traffic department will keep traffic flowing, although there will be some stop signs not justified by traffic flow. There will be compromises between quality and low cost and between the number of machines and professional staff on one hand and the number of unskilled or semi-skilled workers on the other. In any given city, the compromises will occur at different points, favoring either professional or political viewpoints. The achievement of professional goals—not simply bureaucratic goals of increased budget and personnel—can be as expensive as patronage appointments, or lack of technical qualification.

During the years of mounting deficits, the compromises worked out seemed to favor the professionals. In one case, for example, the development department wanted to hire a part-time architect (a professional) to inspect buildings. A council member proposed instead to hire a couple of college students as draftsmen (patronage positions). The Development Department got its part-time architect. Equipment purchases accounted for substantial portions of the annual budgetary increment at the same time that departments resisted patronage personnel. The requests for equipment originated with the departments and were passed with the connivance of the council. For example, one year the council restored to the budget the city manager's cutbacks on heavy equipment.

Pressure for Police Department expansion gave further evidence of both the opposition between professionals and politicians and the tendency for professional solutions to dominate. Councilmen were getting enormous pressure from constituents to expand the Police Department in order to control crime in the streets, whereas the police chief wanted to improve the department's quality. Both the politicians and the professionals agreed to increase the size of the Police Department, but within this agreement, the differing goals of the politicians and professionals were apparent. Politicians wanted foot patrols, officers in visible locations, and police stations in rough black neighborhoods. The Police Department, arguing that it made the men too vulnerable and that black neighborhoods did not have the highest crime rates, resisted these requests. The police chief argued on the basis of staffing levels set by the National Association of Chiefs of Police, standards which, by the way, increased over a ten-year period. The council agreed to the increases, even though they could not affect deployment as much as they wished. The result was increased staffing without patronage.

That the balance between professional and political goals can shift (for many reasons) toward one or the other side is perhaps a weakness in the system. In either case, if the balance shifts too far, the result is liable to be fiscal stress. In one case there may be overeducated personnel, overstaffed departments, and expensive equipment (the newest and best), but little or no patronage. In the other case also, there is apt to be overstaffing, but with underskilled patronage employees. There may be many equipment purchases, but of indifferent quality and unknown vintage. More likely, people will substitute for equipment.

Summary

Based on the analysis in the chapter, we can certainly perceive a kind of vulnerability at Southside's city hall. The city was vulnerable to union demands not just because unions were backed by a groundswell of (white) popular support after the riots, but also because the council refused to make policy concerning personnel. The city staff was unable to take over the council role in making personnel policy. Negotiations were ineptly handled, and the whole personnel question received too little staff attention. Lack of attention to personnel matters reflected council priorities and a general understaffing of managerial functions. The city was vulnerable also in the sense that control over levels of staff depended on a system of balances between professional staff and elected councilmen, a system which broke down during the period of fiscal stress. The professionals brought their own goals to the budgeting process and pressed them with vigor. The reasons for the council's yielding to professional goals will be discussed in the next chapter.

Five

Political Process and Fiscal Stress: Council Behavior

The city council was at the center of political processes in Southside. All major and many minor requests affecting the city had to be passed by the council in public session. No matter where a request originated, it was likely at some time to pass through the city council. Because of limited time and campaign funds, and because of lack of party activity, council meetings were an important way for councilmen to reach the public, especially the politically concerned public who attended council meetings. All of these factors promoted the central position of council meetings in the political process.[1]

Routine issues of subdivision control, zoning appeals, and the like began with conferences between city staff and interested parties, progressed through citizens' committees, and ended before the council as recommendations from both city staff and citizen advisory committees. The city manager was supposed to screen out items which had not been entered through appropriate channels or were not within the jurisdiction of the council. The city manager tended to err on the side of leniency in scheduling individuals to speak; almost anyone who asked eventually came before the council.

Issues could be raised before the council by individuals, by neighborhood associations, or by interest groups, as well as by city departments. Councilmen treated petitioners and homeowners' associations very differently from interest groups. Individuals and neighborhood associations tended to request one-time favors. During the year of the study, actual requests included such items as more police enforcement in given locations, stop signs, permission for special collections for charity, extension of city water and sewer, and exemptions from parking rules. Homeowners' associations were concerned with water-flow, new city projects that impinged on them, sewage treatment, stream cleanup, and the like.

Councilmen generally responded favorably to small requests from constituents except where the cumulative effect of satisfying similar requests would clearly be negative. When councilmen passed these requests to city staff, the staff tried to handle them. The director of the City Water Department, for example, maintained a small staff for the purpose of troubleshooting. One councilman reported that his requests to the departments for such things as cleaning out catchbasins were normally handled within twenty-four hours. Refusal to provide such service was considered a hostile act because it threatened reelection. In the absence of major patronage rewards, such small services became important. The process of granting small favors was public: individuals presented their petitions at council meetings, and the council voted on them in public.

The second way of getting issues before the council was through interest group pressure. The issues involved tended to be of varying scope, and the manner of exerting influence tended to be very diverse. While individuals had one-time favors to ask, the interest groups had long-term, well-focused requests, usually involving large sums of money. Also, instead of requesting single exceptions to rules, they were interested in policy making to protect their welfare.

Interest groups, unlike individual constituents, tended not to appear before the council. Of the four or five interest groups in evidence during the year of the study, only one, the historical preservationists, regularly presented their arguments to the council in public session, and such directness seemed a measure of weakness rather than strength. City staff met privately with the bankers several times during the study to explain and get approval for proposed projects. The downtown businessmen formed a committee that met regularly with city staff while projects were being constructed in order to maintain their input in issues of design change, cost increases, and traffic diversions. The downtown businessmen also maintained a lobbyist who kept up pressure on individual councilmen and maintained constant contact with the city manager (this lobbyist occasionally made presentations to council meetings). The city's unions also tended to work behind the scenes.

One way the interest groups influenced the council was by supporting individual candidates. In the absence of party slating and bloc voting, initial support from interest groups could make a person into a credible candidate. An individual or organization might suggest that someone run or offer to support a candidate, but this did not indicate substantial support.

Both the downtown banks and the unions controlled their candidates on the council rather closely in narrowly defined areas. The unions, for example, expected from their supporters on the council a flow of information in such areas as the contents of discussions at closed door sessions and the true financial picture of the city. They also expected support for their negotiations. The union councilmen acted as liaisons between the council and the unions. The extent to which these union councilmen were bound by specific agreements with the unions became clear when a nonunion councilman proposed a more liberal treatment of the strikers than a union councilman. The union councilman rejected the change and insisted on pushing through the agreement he and the unions had worked out.

The unions' control over the councilmen they helped to elect insured that they got the services they bargained for. Their councilmen benefited from the unions in getting both voters and campaign workers. One union councilman announced shortly after his election that he supported removal of restrictions on city employees to campaign for political candidates. He was striving for a political machine based on city employees, for which he would not trade patronage positions but favorable decisions for the unions.

The unions tight control over two recently elected councilmen and looser control over two other coumcilmen who either sympathized with labor or hoped to gain its electoral support. According to union leadership, the unions had just begun to flex their muscles in political campaigns and would grow more powerful in the future. To illustrate the degree of control they had established, union leadership had managed to mobilize enough union members to knock down an antiunion councilman's name from its traditional first place in the number of votes to third place, within a matter of weeks. Because of this awesome power, the ability of councilmen to act against the unions was limited.

The banks also maintained close ties with "their" councilman. The exchange here was not votes for policy, since the banks did not control a voting bloc. Rather, the banks contributed (1) loans to the city, purchase of bonds and warrants, and (2) the physical maintenance of the downtown through remodeling and rebuilding the banks at private expense. The bankers asked a relative of one of the board members of a downtown bank to run for council. He did, successfully. His set of concerns was so narrowly defined as downtown development that he was not able to appeal to a broad enough constituency to get reelected. However, he did succeed in getting council approval of the downtown development project before he lost his seat.

The implications of this close relation between interest groups and councilmen are complex. Although there was a reformed government with open citizen access, the interest groups continued to be active behind closed doors. Thus, there was a kind of dual system, one public and one less so. The interest groups seemed to perform the role of a party in a more partisan city, but with very narrow constituencies. They chose candidates and offered them financial and in some cases electoral support. Unlike a party, they remained highly fractionated and did not aggregate interests, but because they were the only groups performing these political functions, they exercised considerable influence and were able to get their issues on the agenda.

A second implication is that the currency used for building electoral support and a personal following was pro-union votes rather than job patronage. In a sense, this substitution was more dangerous fiscally than patronage itself. As politicians argue, the numbr of patronage employees can be reduced, whereas union settlements tend to be binding into the future.

The financial importance of the direct ties between interest groups and councilmen should not be overestimated. Most councilmen were not tightly controlled by an interest group, and such controls extended across only a narrowly defined issue area. No councilman appeared to be influenced by more than one interest group. The great electoral power of the city's unions was a developing phenomenon throughout the 1970s. It was not until 1975 that unions actually backed candidates for election, and they failed during their first campaign. Increased union power in campaigns remained a problem for the future but was not the precipitating condition for fiscal stress.

Council Behavior: Ideology, Norms and Resources

The councilmen's values, norms, and resources determined to a large extent how they reacted to citizen and interest group demands once those demnds were on the agenda. Three issues seemed to divide council members: a more or less active or passive concept of their own roles, favorable and unfavorable attitudes towards patronage, and "universalism" or "particularism" in the application of laws.[2] Combining these three aspects of role conception, one can formulate two councilmanic prototypes: (1) the activist, building-oriented type who approves of patronage and believes in particularistic application of the laws; and (2) the nonactivist, anticonstruction type, disapproving of patronage and favoring equal application of the laws. These types come close to representing a reformed and nonreformed perspective on politics.[3]

The first of the three issues which split the council was the extent of a councilman's initiative. In one instance a fight broke out when one councilman, having suggested that a project was not complete without sewers and gutters, proceeded to get estimates for the completion of the project, including price guarantees, and then tried to get the council to vote for the project. A second councilman vehemently opposed this action, not on its merits but because he felt that the first councilman had exceeded the proper councilmanic role. The passive-active dimension came up again, as some councilmembers chastised others for laziness, for not doing their homework, and not doing their share of committee work. For example, one councilman, while admitting that he himself spent too little time on council business, criticized another councilman for spending even less time.

Q: "How many hours would you say you put in on council business each week?"

A: "As few as possible, to be honest. I don't read the material thoroughly, except what directly affects me. Maybe 4–5 hours a week, on a monthly basis, but even that's a lot for no pay. P—— is so hardworking; he spends so much time on it his business is falling apart, and he's going broke. I think the worst councilman is S——. He doesn't even read his agenda before the meeting."

The active-passive dimension of roles was (loosely) associated with a pro-construction or anticonstruction attitude. The more active councilmen usually also expressed an interest in "bricks and mortar." This perspective was reflected in their complaints, such as, "We have the money, but nothing is getting done," or, "No bricks and mortar are going up." This aspect of council activism also surfaced in an interview with the former mayor, who evaluated the successes of his administration in terms of bricks and mortar. The "bricks and mortar" syndrome may also be tied up with career goals of individual councilmen, either in politics or in private life.[4]

A second difference between the councilmen's conceptions of the political process was their tolerance of patronage. Some clearly thought patronage not only acceptable but desirable. In an interview one councilman complained that there was not enough city patronage, making it difficult to reward campaign workers. In a public session another councilman who had continually called for more in-house staff rather than contracting out specialized work, argued for the hiring of more college students for summer work programs. The mayor, by contrast, vehemently opposed patronage jobs at city hall. Other councilmen either were ambivalent or did not indicate their positions by taking revealing stands on issues.

The third and related aspect of the ideological definition of the councilman's role had to do with attitudes towards ordinances and the "universalistic" or "particularistic" application of the laws. Some councilmen made a point of arguing for consistency in application. For example, they almost always voted against "spot zoning" (variances from zoning ordinances for particular cases) and seldom granted builders permission to omit sidewalks (a frequent request). When an event occurred which showed that a law was enforced unequally or was unfair, they argued for suspension of the law until a fairer procedure could be formulated.

For other councilmen the universal application of the law was not particularly important. They argued for humanity in interpretation of the laws and against rigidity. For some of the councilmen, flexibility in application of the laws was a way of saving money because they could accept incomplete bids if lower in price. For others, it was a way of avoiding giving the award to the lowest bidder and of giving it to someone else for political or personal reasons.

Because councilmen differed in their role conception, the council, depending on which coalition was stronger, vacillated between small construction projects for apparently political purposes and inactivity. It fell to outside agencies and the city manager to estimate needs on the basis of city functions. Until imposed by the EPA, basic capital expenditures for sewage disposal were not made. In 1972 the city manager established a program of scheduled (rather than piecemeal) resurfacing of downtown streets. The program was expensive and probably contributed to the deficits in the Streets Department, but it was necessitated by neglect and by the small, erratic projects favored by the council. The city had a difficult time during inflation in carrying out both scheduled maintenance and politically chosen small projects.

Councilmembers observed a norm of reciprocity which required that they be lenient with each others' requests for special projects or special favors. As one councilman put it:

> If someone feels strongly on an issue, if others don't have strong feelings on the issue, that's the way they'll vote. And there's an unwritten rule that if something is in a councilman's district, we'll go along and scratch each other's back. Sometimes if its important, I call them and they ask, "Is this really important to you, Joe?" and I'll say, "This guy is really hurting, and even

though it might cost us a few bucks, that is, cost the city a few bucks, I think we should do it."

The city manager was aware of these norms and the potential burden it put on him. In an interview, he described the fiscal impact of reciprocity in the following terms: "Say they each have a project that costs $450,000, and they defer to each other—the total could blow the budget sky high." Even among political opponents, the norm of reciprocity was strong and made it difficult for the professionals to control the dollar amounts associated with the council's projects.

Though the councilmen adhered to norms of reciprocity, they did not have as many resources as the preceding discussion might imply. For example, they had virtually no paying jobs to dispense. They did, however, control some resources which, with skill, could be turned into political support.[5] These included appointments to boards and committees, awarding bids for city contracts, information, granting favors or exceptions to rules, use of the bureaucracy to solve constituents' problems, special projects, and salary and benefit increases for city workers.

The only kind of "jobs" councilmen had to dispense were unpaid appointments to city commissions. One councilman complained that such honorary positions were their only way to reward campaign workers, and the mayor was not even consulting them on appointments. Over the course of the study, the council did manage to get the mayor to consult with them. This meant that each councilmember could make one or two appointments. At one point in the study, a small special commission to support a new park was suddenly increased from three members to twelve, which illustrated the pressure to increase the number of appointments available.

Appointments to city commissions were rewards to campaign workers, but they were also a way of controlling the political process. For the mayor in particular, who lacked both extensive legal power and the power of personality, commission appointments were his way of ensuring that like-minded citizens would be making recommendations to the council. In a controversy over the construction of parking decks, for example, he appointed a well-known opponent of the decks to the parking commission in the hopes that the commission's negative recommendation would be sustained by the council. The mayor would thus gain control of the outcome. The mayor's minority faction in Southside controlled many appointments, although the council majority was usually able to overturn commission recommendations, nullifying the commissions' influence.

Appointments to committees on the council were also a political resource. Appointments were the exclusive prerogative of the mayor, and this was one of his few tools to forge a coalition on the council. The mayor tried to win support for his anti-parking-deck position by promising appointments on the highly desirable finance committee. Of the two councilmen who voted with him, one did so for his own ideological reasons. The other was promised and given an appointment on the finance committee.

A second type of resource was the awarding of bids to private businesses. The eagerness of some councilmen to build things and the peculiar inability of the council to come to a compromise on the parking decks indicated some kind of favoritism on contracts for construction. Even the councilmen themselves accused each other of favoritism in letting bids, especially when they opposed the project. Out-and-out corruption of this sort seemed quite limited. One councilman noted, "In a city manager government there is less opportunity for illegitimate contracts, except, perhaps for the city manager, and even he is pretty much under the surveillance of the city council."

The one area where it is not clear whether there was corruption was in letting bids when the lowest bid was not accepted. This is a common enough occurrence in city governments, but in Southside the reasons for not giving the award to the lowest bidder were not always clear. The bidders had gotten so frustrated by city practices that many of them did not bid at all. While this also happened occasionally in other cities, it had reached crisis proportions in Southside. A council committee was formed to investigate and recommend new bidding procedures. A meeting was held at city hall of local businessmen to find out why they were not bidding. Some argued that the paperwork and legal requirements were burdensome, but the overall consensus was that the city's past inconsistency, sometimes giving the award to the low bidder and sometimes not, made them feel the bidding procedure was illegitimate. They asked only for consistency.

Scaring away bidders through inconsistency is costly in itself. The bidding procedure can be effective only if several bidders are trying to outdo each other to get the bid. With no bidders, only one bidder, or constant rebidding, the price of city purchases is bound to increase. How much of this inconsistency was due to councilmen's efforts to award the bids selectively and how much extra the city might have paid on bids is not clear. Councilmen did not develop either an outright pattern of favoritism or one of standard review. Their inconsistency certainly reduced the number of bidders and probably raised costs.

Based on the responses of one councilman, the bidding companies assumed that the councilmen had the ability to award the bids to one company or another and so put pressure on individual councilmen. This evidence is consistent with the opinions announced at the meeting of potential bidders. The exact extent to which councilmen responded to this pressure is unclear. The mayor and one councilman fought over whether bids should be awarded to companies outside the city limits. The norm of awarding bids to companies within the city limits contradicted the principle of accepting the lowest bidder and thus probably increased prices somewhat. The councilman who argued that they could go outside if there were no internal bidders was himself interested in a political career outside the city. The rest of the council's emotional support for the principle of awarding the bid inside the city indicates at least some yielding to the pressures of local companies. Another sign that councilmembers might be using bids politically was the award of the garbage pickup contract to a company with suspected underworld connections. This contract was considerably more expensive for city residents than comparable services in other cities.

The entire bidding procedure was inefficient. The reason for not taking the lowest bid varied from incomplete bids to weak economic backing of the company making the bid, from poor past performance to being outside the city (and thus less able to provide service). But once the door was open to rejecting the lowest bid, the criteria for choice were no longer clear to the public or the bidders. Widespread belief that bids were subject to favoritism was sufficient to raise city costs and political allocation of bid awards increased them further.

Besides appointments and bids, councilmen had valuable information. Union councilmen were expected to pass on to the unions information gained from closed door sessions, budget transactions, and the like. Councilmen also gave information to reporters in exchange for coverage (presumably favorable). The financial impact of these exchanges of information is impossible to assess. The ability of the unions to assess precisely what cost level the city might be willing to settle on and how various councilmen stood on the bargaining undoubtedly gave an advantage to the unions. Whether or not councilmen enabled others to make money on land deals by revealing the future location of city facilities is not known, but was suspected (the amount of land held by banks in blind trust makes tracing such deals exceedingly difficult).

A fourth resource available to councilmen was granting exceptions to rules. A petitioner requesting rezoning, exception from parking rules, free water hookups, or exemption from sidewalks, subdivision controls, or the like might come before the council. Since rezoning, subdivisons, and exemption from rules adds greatly to the value of a property or reduces costs to the petitioner at no dollar cost to the city, this kind of favor was easy to grant. However, overriding the city's rules can cause considerable chaos and can lead to charges of favoritism or unequal application of the laws.

A fifth resource of councilmen was the use of the city's departments to solve individual constituent's problems and provide special services. Some departments were more responsive to these kinds of requests than others. Sewer and Water was geared to troubleshoot for councilmen. So, to some extent, was Public Works, including Streets, although they tended to respond more slowly than Sewer and Water. Police seemed to resist councilmanic requests over a long period of time. They resisted the mayor's request for a police substation in a poor part of town (because the crime rate was not high enough to justify it) requests by a councilman for more visible foot patrol in the downtown area (not enough money in the budget).

The direct dollar cost of using city agencies to provide favors was not great. In departments which complied with councilmen's requests, it meant a different internal organization and perhaps more contracting out of work. But these departments rejected councilmanic pressures to add more employees so their requests could be filled more promptly. The department heads feared patronage appointments to the new slots and getting stuck year-round with specialized employees whom they would then have to keep busy by creating new projects. This outcome is counterintuitive because it violates the dictum that a bureaucrat always wants to specialize and expand his personnel. It shows a distinction between bureaucratic expansion and professionalism. Because of the professionals' resistance to new positions, the total number of favors done for councilmen had to be limited, and the cost probably was not great.

Another major resource for councilmen was the projects that they voted for. The city manager openly blamed their special projects for fiscal stress and described them as unsound. Their cost, as well as their type and scope, proved financially draining. They tended to be small projects which would benefit one neighborhood or one group of people. They were always highly visible and in areas of high public demand. Less visible projects, such as water and sewer improvements, were not included, which is why the water system was allowed to deteriorate. The projects also tended by their nature to be piecemeal, and diverted funds from routine maintenance to special projects. Individual councilmen could then take credit for a project, which they could not do if routine maintenance steadily progressed under the control of department heads.

The councilmen's use of projects to draw attention to themselves helped shape the pattern of fiscal stress. Over a long period of time, basic services and capital projects necessary for the functioning and attractiveness of the city were neglected. The chickens came home to roost in the 1970s when maintenance and new construction was no longer avoidable.

One additional resource of the councilmen was favorable action toward the city unions. Due to the lack of patronage and the decline in bloc voting, the support of the city's unions had become increasingly important. The inability of the council to control the unions and give the city negotiating team clear guidance was due partly to inexperience but also partly to the desire of some councilmen to court, or appear to court, the unions. According to a union negotiator, several councilmen actually encouraged the unions to stay out on strike and hold out for a higher cash settlement. The lack of firm policy led to expensive settlements with the unions. These costs were cumulative from year to year (though smaller on an annual basis than the size of the deficits).

In summarizing the impact of the ideological splits, norms, and resources of city councilmen, one overriding condition must be kept in mind: the coalition supporting the city manager system was only partly successful in electing councilmen who felt that public service was a burdensome civic obligation. Also on the council were members who enjoyed politics and wanted a political career. They wanted to be reelected, but as this list of resources suggests, they had limited means with which to build a following. They were consequently vulnerable to demands on the one hand and eager to get special projects into the budget on the other.[6]

The Politics of the Budgetary Process[7]

Up to this point, the political process has been described in some detail. The link between politics and deficits is the budget. Budgeting reflects the entire political process in microcosm and shows more clearly than any other feature of the political system how a city incurs deficits.

In order to reconstruct the budget process, most meetings on the budget were observed throughout one budget cycle. The observations took place in 1976, one year after the height of deficits and after the beginning of budget retrenchment. Budgetary procedures were not uniform from year to year, so the procedures observed were not necessarily the ones used during the most acute buildup of financial stress. But the budgetary process in 1976 provided important clues as to what occurred in prior years. Also, deficits were still occurring in 1976, so it was possible to observe how the deficits were budgeted in that year.

The budgetary process followed the formal procedures of departmental request, executive review, and council appropriation only in a general way, with the following stages: (1) The budget process began with a meeting of the department heads and the city manager to discuss procedures and to set the tone for the request. (2) The departments then drew up requests. (3) The requests were processed, and cut back, by the city manager. (4) From there they went normally to the finance committee, consisting of the finance director and two councilmen, who reviewed the budgets. (5) Then the requests were presented to the whole council in informal session by the city manager. (6) The appropriations were then approved by the council. (7) The council met with department heads to discuss ongoing or new projects. (8) Still later the council met to order priorities within the appropriations (see table 5.1).

The budgetary process was more complicated than even such a long list of stages would suggest. There were more actors at each stage than this list would suggest, and some actors played dual roles. Budget proposals sometimes went back and forth between steps before moving on. Sometimes the steps were merged or occurred almost simultaneously. Any notion that the budget was processed in a neat sequence of steps would be too simplistic.[8]

The first steps in the budget process were the early meeting of the department heads and the city manager and the drawing up of departmental requests. Where the process became complicated was in the evaluation stages. The city manager described these steps in some detail:

> The requests from the department are done on extensively detailed forms, in which we ask the names of each personnel member, his salary, anticipated increases, such as step raises, and justification of every item of expense, with perhaps a small margin for unplanned, but fairly predictable items like trips to the State Capitol. *When we get these requests, we juggle them a bit and do our thing, and pass on the recommendations.* . . . If settlement [with the unions] occurs between the time when the departments

Table 5.1
The Budget Process

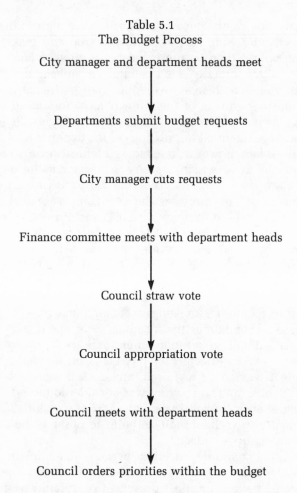

City manager and department heads meet

Departments submit budget requests

City manager cuts requests

Finance committee meets with department heads

Council straw vote

Council appropriation vote

Council meets with department heads

Council orders priorities within the budget

return their forms and the time I submit the budget, then my estimates will be a little higher than the departments'. If settlement occurs after I submit the budget the council will raise my estimates.

The city manager's version of the budget request and evaluation stage implies that all expenditures not justified by precise formulae would be cut, but that, in general, the city manager would pass on the departments' budgets for council approval. In actuality, (1) the city manager had no precise formulae for evaluating personnel and equipment requests ("we juggle them a bit"); (2) he did not always get to review the budget proposal earlier than the city council members; and (3) he did not have a free hand in cutting back budget requests.

As formally set up, the department heads were to meet first with the city manager, who would go over the proposal and make a cut version, which would then be presented to the finance committee. The finance committee formally acted as a liaison between the city finance director and the council in allowing the finance director to communicate with those members of the council most interested in finance. The committee had no power to cut or restore budgets. Its formal role was to report back general impressions of the departments' requests to the council. In fact, however, it acted as a budget review committee.

The formal plan in which the city manager cut the departments' requests before the preliminary hearing with the finance committee did not work out uniformly, as the city manager had the flu for a week, and it turned out the department heads did not know this was the proper sequence (at least that is what they reported to me). Some departments thus were cut first and then met with the finance committee to discuss the budget; others met with the committee first, then went to the city manager, and finally went back to the committee with a cut version.

The finance committee meetings were a crucial stage in the budget review process. Sometimes the meetings were open, with the mayor and the press attending, but more often there were two council members, the city finance director, the city manager, the department head whose budget was being reviewed, and myself. Sometimes the city manager was absent. The meeting was considered closed if the press was not there, even though I was present. Consequently, these meetings provided an excellent vantage point to observe the political aspects of drawing up a budget.

In general, the committee meetings began with an opening presentation of the department head. The presentation offered a potpourri of budget details, defenses against presumed complaints against the department, and proposed solutions of such problems. A common defensive presentation was "the budget is not padded—there is no place to cut." Department heads maintained they never submitted padded budgets, even though the city manager had just cut out some obvious padding. One department head compared his new, leaner budget to the old days when departments had to pad because budgets were routinely cut 50%.

About two-thirds of the way into each meeting, department heads began to introduce "dreams," pet projects for which they hoped to get council approval. The opportunity to talk directly to councilmen and bypass the city manager was so appealing none could resist it. Sometimes the requests were tentative; sometimes they were bolder.

The Police Department's request was one that went to the finance committee before it went to the city manager. In this session, the "dreams" portion was very bold. The police chief mentioned the desire for more space for his expanded police force—new lockers, showers, and the like. When the finance director asked for an estimate of cost, the chief was not only able to produce detailed cost estimates but also blueprints. The councilmen were enthusiastic, and *encouraged him also to think about building a station at the new shopping mall;* he said he was thinking about it, and *they decided it should be a shared facility with the Fire Department.* They called in the fire chief and discussed it with him, and *they decided to refer it back to the city manager "with enthusiasm."* When the councilmen and the budget officer met with the department head before the city manager had seen the request, they unanimously encouraged the inclusion of a new, expensive project in the budget request. They expanded on the "dream" and then referred the proposal back to the city manager in such a way that he would know that it had at least partial backing by the council.

The arguments used by the department heads to justify their requests were primarily professional and technical. The police and fire chiefs both argued that they needed new expenditures in order to operate more efficiently. The police chief referred to standards set by professional associations. The director of the Sewer and Water Department argued that he wanted the *best* (my italics), and that if he requested something it was because he had to have it.

Besides professional arguments of national standards, quality, and other technical requirements to make something work, the department heads also used other arguments. One referred to what other cities and what the county was doing. The director of Sewer and Water maintained that, though his operation was seldom visible, if it did not work and sewage backed up, the councilmen would hear from constituents. He also contended (in terms of time horizons) that the city was living off the depreciation in its water system.

At the same time the finance committee was evaluating the budget and listening to the department heads defending it, they also explored solutions to increased costs in many areas, such as insurance, workmen's compensation, and automobile maintenance. One councilman questioned the promotion and position structure in the Police Department, and the issue was thoroughly aired with the city manager, finance director, chief of police, and the councilmen, all discussing the ideas and implications.

The city manager objected to the proposal for a new position structure because it violated union contracts. He argued that many of the solutions being discussed violated the contract and would affect negotiations. The councilmen seemed ignorant of the provisions of the contract. Although the city manager was concerned with the upcoming negotiations and the impact of the proposed budget on those negotiations, the budget officer took the stance that everything should be open and that whatever money was available would go to the unions for salary increase. This stance was taken to please the councilmembers—their projects first, the leftover to the unions. In the end that is what was done. Instead of keeping secret the amount available and negotiating about it, the sum left over was put in the budget for salary increases. It may have pleased the council, but it did not please the unions.

After the hearings with the budget committee, the departments' requests went before the whole council in informal session. The process of the preliminary hearings was repeated, except that the impressions of the finance committee had been conveyed to the whole council. (The content of their recommendations is unknown to me.) The city manager, reading the line items of each department from a computer printout, explained them in detail. Councilmen questioned both increases and decreases and asked about budget items they did not understand with such queries as "why does it cost this much to feed prisoners?" and "who pays for towing parked cars?" Sometimes the city manager, sometimes the department head, would answer the questions.

At the last of this second set of meetings the city manager introduced two memos, one concerning a proposed grantsman, suggested by the two councilmen on the finance committee, and a second incorporating the mayor's desire to develop a new personnel office. The proponents of the two ideas were direct antagonists on the council. To make matters worse, the proposals evoked ideological opposition was well, since the grantsman was to get federal monies for the city, which the mayor opposed on principle, and the personnel office was intended to control patronage, an issue which also divided the council. The two proposals were made at the same time. The mayor voiced his opposition to the grantsman but accepted the position as a quid pro quo to get his personnel officer.

The next major budget meeting followed shortly after the last council budget meeting. The mayor asked the city manager for departmental reports on their budget increases from 1964 to 1976. Four or five days later the city manager received these reports and distributed copies for discussion to the council. Each department had to present to the council the amount of and reasons for increases over time.

Then a public hearing was held on revenue sharing funds. Since the money had already been committed by the finance director, the meeting was unnecessary for decision making but was required by law. Representatives of groups made their pleas. The finance director announced that all the money was going to the Fire Department because of the financial situation and that the council had decided to do this with the federal money, at least until the city achieved a balanced budget. At each presentation the city manager asked questions on alternative sources of funding and whether the money was to be used for special projects or ongoing support. At several points the finance officer cut in to establish that the group had received considerable money in the past, as if that were sufficient reason for not giving aid. The groups requesting funds performed quasi-public functions, such as aiding drug abusers, physically handicapped, and the poor.

After the revenue sharing meeting, the next stage was the passage of the budget itself. In the past this had been troublesome because councilmen who opposed one portion of the budget voted against the whole document. To prevent its defeat, the council had taken straw votes on controversial items. Items rejected would not appear in the budget. When the final vote was to be taken, each councilman could express his opposition for the record without rejecting the whole budget. In the end the budget passed with only one negative vote.

The new budget contained a 7% addition for salary increases. Union leaders attending the council meeting had left in a huff because they felt that the city was trying to legislate salary increases instead of bargaining. The firemen went on strike over the issue and managed to pull out another union (AFSCME), with the police union on standby to go out if necessary. The strike lasted more than a week, although an injunction was sought after several days. The judge took no action on the injunction and forced both sides to bargain. The final settlement called for a salary increase of 8.5%, although the city had determined it had only 7% available. The increase was, therefore, delayed until the following year.

After the budget was approved, it had to be administered. The budget appropriated is seldom the budget expended, especially in capital items. The city had no separate capital budget, no list of departmental priorities. What money would actually be released, for what purpose and when, was at the discretion of the finance director. The order in which projects were done could be affected (if not totally determined) by the staff. Councilmen who had managed to get projects into the budget only to find them continually shifted to lowest priority could lose them entirely. Vigilance was in order, and a moderate amount of harassment of department heads by councilmen went on. During the year of the study the council was given a formal opportunity to determine the priorities of projects after the budget was passed. However, at this meeting, the city staff first ordered the projects on the basis of the percentage of state or federal funding and the proportion already completed. The council did not have much leeway with their own priorities after these conditions were met.

After the budget was passed, the council had a long meeting to get updates on the projects of all the departments. While some of these sounded more like personnel requests, overall the procedure was very like a verbal program budget. Projects were discussed, progress explored, future desirability examined. Departments used the sessions as opportunities to brag about accomplishments or plead for approval of bids or contracts necessary to carry out the projects. These sessions should be viewed as part of the budgetary process, both because they affected expenditures and because they provided another direct point of contact between the council and the department heads.

Weaknesses in the Budgetary Process

How do deficits occur in the budgetary process? Is the city manager not playing his role of budget cutter properly? Did the council override the city manager's recommendations? Was there some weakness in the budgetary process itself?

First, the roles of the various actors can be inferred from the hearings. The budget officer and the councilmen seemed to be playing double roles, sometimes encouraging and sometimes curtailing expenditures. The city manager seemed to have a relatively consistent but ineffective role of budgetary watchdog.

The budget officer's role was at variance with that appropriate to the staff of an expenditure-controlling city manager. The budget officer encouraged the dreams of the department heads and even suggested new projects. He encouraged a stance that would please the councilmembers but alienate the unions, with a possibly unsettling effect on the budgetary balance. From time to time, however, he reminded department heads and councilmen about revenue limitations, particularly in the operating rather than in the capital budget. (There was no capital budget as such. Capital items were listed as an expense category in the operating budget, but since they were grouped separately, it was possible to categorize them and analyze them.)

In a strategic move, the budget director tried to consolidate his own support with the department heads and the council and to exacerbate relations between them and the city manager by forcing the latter to cut back on the fat he (the budget officer) had just put in. By alienating labor he precipitated a strike for which the city manager was blamed and consequently fired. Presumably this was the budget director's goal, since he had apparently sought the position when the assistant city manager was made manager in 1972. Despite his maneuvers, he still had to play the role of budget director in order to take credit for turning around the fiscal crisis. Thus he reminded them all of revenue limitations.

The role of the two councilmembers on the finance committee was also rather complex. On the one hand, they listened carefully to justification of increases in such a way that they could explain them to the council. Without formal authority to approve or disapprove, they tried to discourage the departments from restoring all the employees they had cut the previous year because it would look silly in front of the whole council. Their behavior implied that such replacement was okay with them but that the council would never accept it. In curbing the departments, the committee councilmen felt curtailed in their own projects and felt too constrained in their dealings with the departments. They would have liked being more generous. As a result, they recommended to the Development Department that it hire a grantsman to increase the amount of revenue available. The finance committee members, themselves activists on the council, thus were responsible for initiating a new position in a departmental request. They also encouraged the Police Department's requests for more space.

Although the budget officer and the councilmembers had mixed roles, the city manager's role was more consistent even if less effective. He tried to cut expenses, but he had difficulty, especially when it was made clear to him that projects he wished to cut had councilmanic backing. For example, the police chief had spoken about his request with the city manager. The city manager cut out several personnel and a new project. When the police chief came back for a second meeting with the finance committee, the city manager tried to cut still another item, the shooting range. When one of the councilmen objected, the manager then backed down slightly, saying, "At least I'll cut most of it." This exchange illustrates the relationship between the councilmembers and the departments, or at least with the police chief. Special projects were agreed to and put in the budget request. The city manager's job of cutting fat and producing a balanced budget put him in the position of trying to cut out some, if not all, councilmanic pet projects. This was very difficult to do.

In short, no actor played out the ideal role spelled out in the city manager prototype. The steps of proposal, review, and approval were clear, but the role of actors at each stage was muddled. The city manager was not free to cut and could not act independently of the council. Councilmembers acted not as a rubber stamp at the end but as proposers of projects in the early phases of budget review. The city finance director also acted out contradictory roles. These lapses from the standard suggested something drastically wrong with the budget process.

Not only were the actors' roles wrong, but the sequence of steps was out of order. Sometimes the departments got a chance to present their budget to the council committee before the city manager had seen it. Sometimes they were able to plead with individual council members to overturn the city manager's cuts before the budget went to the whole council. Councilmembers also went directly to the city manager with pet projects before the budget was trimmed (this information came from an interview with the city manager). Instead of a sequence in which departments dealt with the city manager, who then dealt with the council, the departments frequently contacted the council. As a result, councilmen's pet projects appeared in departmental budgets, and the city manager was informed what he should not cut. Thus council members owed favors to the department heads which might be repaid by leniency toward purely departmental requests. The city manager could cut pet projects only meagerly for fear of alienating councilmembers. The whole process had become political rather than administrative and diminished the possibility of applying controls.

When the former city manager was interviewed six months after the firemen's strike (and after his subsequent firing), he was asked about the budget process during his term in office. He replied that he had provided the department heads many opportunities to meet with the council. His hope was that the department heads would learn that their requests had to be accommodated into a broader framework of other departmental requests and the overall good of the city. So much contact with the council had turned out to be a mistake, he felt, because it politicized the budget process. The political relations between the departments and the council observed in 1976 were thus the results of a conscious policy decision on the part of the city manager. This policy dates at least as far back as 1973 when it was announced in the budget preface, and it probably goes back to 1972 and the beginning of the deficits.

In short, effective city manager government is dependent on having a council restrained from pursuing pet projects and/or a budgetary process which really isolates the department heads from the council.

The department heads may then still be powerful and make excessive demands, but without council backing, the city manager can cut their budgets. In Southside, the city manager claims he purposely brought the department heads and the council together, but it appears that in fact he did not have the power to keep them apart. In either case, once they got together they forged a coalition that he was not strong enough to restrain. The split council kept him weak. This would not have been so harmful except for the councilmen's pet projects.

Some fundamental inadequacies in the budgetary process extended back to the beginning period of deficits. Also some costly temporary problems appeared in the 1976 budget cycle, but they were not endemic to the budgetary process. The entire budgetary process was completed before the union negotiations on monetary issues began. The pet projects of the councilmen were included in the budget, and the remaining unappropriated revenue was budgeted for salary increases. By leaving union negotiations instead of councilmanic projects to the end of the allocation process, the city gave the councilmen no incentive to economize. If their own projects had come last, councilmen might have trimmed the allocations to departments and unions, to insure that there was some money left for themselves. But once their projects were safely in the budget, they cared less if the departments got too much money and the unions, last on the list, were left with too little. Thus the council created the possibility of a strike and a deficit if the settlement exceeded the budgeted amount for salary increases. The initial inclusion of pet projects, despite the implications for finance, was a result of direct relations between the city's staff, in this case the finance director, and the city councilmen. In a sense, then, this problem too was a reflection of the more general problem of too much direct contact between department heads and the council.

Budgeting and the Political Process

The budgetary process exemplified many of the issues described earlier. For example, the alliance between the department heads and the city council finance committee illustrated the overall weakness of the city manager. His inability to cut back certain budget requests resulted from his inexperience on the one hand and the split council on the other. Councilmen told him what items not to cut, and he was plainly risking his job if he ignored the advice.

The kinds of requests made by department heads and the kinds of projects advocated by councilmembers illustrated the basic opposition between professional and political goals. Department heads requested excellent equipment and defended personnel requests in terms of national (professional) standards. Councilmembers argued for bricks and mortar projects; for example, they rejected a plan for free space for a police substation in favor of a proposal involving capital outlay. Councilmen encouraged police expansion into an unused warehouse and supported the creation of a gun practice range, even over the city manager's objections. In each instance there was evidence of councilmen trading off support for budget items with the department heads (if I protect your gun range, you allow me to put a capital project in your request).

The priority of special requests of the "bricks and mortar" type in councilmanic decision making illustrates not only the ideological typology developed in this chapter but also other portions of the political process. The firemen went out on strike because the finance committee budgeted first for special projects and gave only the remainder, prior to bargaining, to the unions. This decision could have been politically disastrous. To avoid the consequences of their decision, they blamed the city manager for the strike and fired him. Then the whole council publicly took a lenient stance toward the strikers. The councilmen's dependence on union votes dictated their public leniency toward the unions and their scapegoating the city manager. Because they systematically shifted the blame for poor personnel relations to the city manager they helped to erode his power base. Moreover, the councilmen on the finance committee were not "bound" by the unions. During the budget hearings they showed considerable ignorance of contract provisions, and they put their own special projects before the union settlement.

Significant also is the role of public and pressure groups in the budgetary process. There was only one genuinely public meeting, the revenue sharing hearing, outside regular council meetings and budget sessions. Organized agencies serving the poor and ill attended that meeting to make requests for funds. The decision on how the money would be spent had already been made, so the finance director and the city manager treated the requests in a somewhat cavalier fashion. The requests had no impact on administrative decisions. Beyond this single meeting, neither the public nor interest groups had any direct impact on the budgetary process. The only outsiders admitted to the preliminary budget hearings were county officials and the press, neither of whom represented either citizens or interest groups. The interest groups were therefore dependent on their council representatives to argue for their projects. If they had no representative on the finance committee, they were at a disadvantage. Although council meetings were open to the public and individuals could easily present petitions, individual citizens had little *direct* impact on the budget.

Summary

In this and the preceding chapter it has been shown that the South-side's political system, independent of underlying social and economic conditions, both shaped and contributed to fiscal stress. Central to that system was a competition between reformed and nonreformed government. The particular compromises struck between the two systems were not financially stable. Actors were unable or unwilling to perform their assigned roles at assigned times. The city manager was too weak to cut the budgets, there was too much contact between the department heads and the council, and there were too few resources for politically ambitious councilmen to build a following. As a result of the combination of political ambitions and lack of patronage, councilmen became increasingly dependent on interest groups such as banks and unionized employees and insistent on putting special projects in the budget. In exchange for permission to put their projects into the departmental budgets, they approved the departments' expansion plans. The department heads' norms of professionalism and the council's norms of reciprocity made the projects especially costly. Ideological splits on the council left the city with cycles of under- and overenforcement of ordinances and alternation between no capital projects and small separable projects. Consequently, areal growth was severely undercapitalized. Many of these aspects of political behavior were apparent not just during council meetings but also in the budgetary process.

Six

Causes and Responses to Fiscal Stress: Their Interactions over Time

The local political structure of Southside was the context for the occurrence of fiscal problems, but not the necessary and sufficient condition required to create it. Fiscal stress was a complex amalgam of national forces and local conditions, of economic and political trends as they intertwined over the years. It was also the result of independent changes occurring at the same time, and the result of emotion being turned into institutional arrangements, locking up larger and larger pieces of the problem. The very efforts taken to ameliorate the problems seemed to exacerbate them.

The Actors' Explanations of Fiscal Stress

Nearly all the actors at city hall played some role in the generation of deficits. Also, they observed the process closely enough to know what happened in areas outside their own. They were highly knowledgeable about what happened and at the same time eager to deflect blame from themselves. Their answers to "What caused fiscal stress?" were almost uniformly correct in identifying some portion of the problem, but, depending on their role at city hall, they often identified a different portion. Politicians emphasized one set of factors, city staff a second set, and union representatives a third. Also, actors at city hall never suggested interactions between factors over time.

This section will examine the actors' explanations for the causes of fiscal stress. It will discuss first the reasons given by the politicians, then by the professional staff, and finally by the union negotiators.

The politicians, evasive about the causes of fiscal stress, tended either to minimize its importance or to blame it on national trends over which the city had no control. For example, the former mayor (in office from 1960–1972) while identifying many actual causes of deficits, tended to blame outsiders and deny his own responsibility. He noted that the city increased the number of police from eighty to two hundred during his administration. He argued that inflation had taken a big bite from local revenues. The price of fire trucks went from twenty-five thousand dollars to seventy-five thousand dollars while he was in office. He also indicated that there had been a gradual increase in scope of city government, which formerly had provided only sewer and water service and relied on volunteer firemen and policemen. Later, cities got involved in housing, transportation, and many other things. He argued that citizens were not willing to pay for these services because the total tax bite became so great. He observed that patronage and corruption is worse at the federal than the local level. Moreover, civil service prevented incompetents from being fired or told what to do. He preferred patronage appointees because they can be fired. He also argued that the federal government takes more in taxes than it returns to the cities and then will not bail out the cities.

When the former mayor was asked why "the police force tripled [a slight exaggeration], and salaries doubled" (his phrase), he responded, "because of violence and crime—police training, antibrutality training, hiring more officers, and so on. Then the officers say it's risky. They want more money. They have taken advantage of the disorder."

The former mayor went on to specify the size of cities and the deterioration of the sense of community as the causes of the problem. He took a defensive stand: "No one individual can control this. The mayor didn't do it. What happened to the social fabric? The mayor or the governor can't do it."

Preferring to dwell on concepts of relative deprivation, the former mayor only reluctantly related the increased crime rates to the changing ethnic composition of the city. He was singularly tight-lipped on the riots themselves and offered only that those blacks he dealt with were drunken rabble-rousers from outside the city. Curiously, the mayor did indicate that the city's fire and police force took advantage of the civil unrest to press their claims for higher salaries. But when asked "What do you think accounted for the increase in union militance?" he immediately cited national trends:

It's not just here. We have a half dozen goliaths who can paralyze society. Huge corporations. Fifty years ago we had no unions;

now major unions can stop the economy. Unions are just imitating other unions."

While the former mayor diverted the blame, he did not minimize the seriousness of fiscal stress or its causes. Other political figures handled the blame by minimizing the importance of fiscal stress. Two councilmen who started their terms in the middle of the crisis period argued that fiscal stress was just an accounting problem. They implied that the budget was set up in such a way that the occurrence and importance of deficits was not clear. These same two councilmen also argued that the state had forced the city to increase its contributions to the pension funds and that these two factors together caused the deficits.

A former councilman in office when the financial problems began likewise minimized the importance of the fiscal stress. His first response was, "Tell me a city that isn't traditionally in trouble." He described the legal limits imposed on police and fire pension funds. According to his argument, the rate of taxation and of payout was mandated by the state, so the deficits were entirely beyond their control. Other funds, he maintained, were sound. He also noted that contingencies such as snowfall or damburst during the year could throw off the budget. As an example of unanticipated cost increases he cited a sudden rise in insurance rates during the year. At another point in the interview, he injected the idea that people ask the government to do more now than in the past, because "we raised a generation on welfare."

Politicians provided a very limited view of the city's financial problems. They tended to exonerate themselves and blame trends over which they had no control. They minimized their own discretion. A local riot with immediate impact on the city was referred to as civil unrest, relating it to the national scene. According to the politicians, local unions were responding to national unions, and inflation (impersonal, uncontrollable) was the cause of rising costs. Outsiders—the state and the federal government—rioters—aggravated matters.

In contrast, the city staff did not minimize the fiscal problems, and they focused almost entirely on matters internal to the city. Some, like the city planners, took a technical view of problems. The planners argued that revenue was too low because of the city's persistently low tax base compared with cities of comparable size. Also, the city had unfortunately annexed a great deal of land without regard to cost and in a piecemeal fashion, leading to pockets which were difficult to serve. Their solution was to annex more businesses, which would provide more revenue than they cost in services. They viewed the

problems in terms of the routine business of the planning office—
land use, annexations, revenue generated, and services extended.

The city manager, while incorporating the basic interpretations of
the planners, gave a much broader analysis that still focused on the
city. He argued that the city had remained dormant too long, and that
the first attempts to develop it had been clumsy. It had grown considerably in population and area, and now the government had to cope
with that growth.

In addition to citing the effects of prior underinvestment, and prior
growth, the city manager blamed many local actors. He blamed the
city council for raising his budget twice during his years in office, the
unions and the courts for heavy labor settlements, and his own and
his budget officer's lack of experience in 1972. He blamed the county
for holding onto revenues and forcing the city to borrow. He also
mentioned many inefficient city operations that could have been done
better on a regional basis or in cooperation with other governments.
He readily admitted to budgetary practices such as sliding deficits
forward and borrowing between funds. He argued that once the size of
a deficit was discovered, he could not reduce it all at once for fear of
losing his job. When asked whether the department heads had contributed to the deficits, he said he thought so because they had refused
to make the cuts he requested and preferred to shift the blame onto
him. When he then made the cuts, they were infuriated and met
together in the hope of getting him fired. Although the city manager
implicated everyone—unions, management, the council, and the department heads—like the rest of the staff he did not try to blame
trends, inflation or outsiders, except for the county pattern of disbursing revenues. He tried occasionally to shift the blame from himself
onto the finance director or the council or a judge, but he focused
primarily on the city itself.

The city finance director indicated that the problem was not a
superficial cash flow problem, but the result of expenditures outrun-
ning revenues. A tax increase was needed. He implied that the council
had to be instructed on the necessity of a tax increase and had to be
shielded from the heat generated by that action. Implicit in his analysis was that the councilmen's political vulnerability brought about
the deficits because of their reluctance to raise taxes. On being pressed
for what he thought had pushed expenditures up, and whether the
city might be overstaffed or paying too high salaries, he suggested that
the Police Department might be overstaffed because of too many
highly trained technicians such as electricians and too many highly
paid assistants to the chief. He also pointed out the problem of uncon-

trollable overtime due to court procedures. The finance director explicitly denied that there had been any overestimation of revenues. He indicated that the police and fire pension funds had been chronically underfunded but, until pressed, would not talk about the state pension fund for other city employees. Then he indicated (with considerable discomfort) that it had been subsidized by other funds and should probably have its own tax.

In short, the finance director did not try to minimize the seriousness of the deficits, nor did he try to blame outside agents or inevitable cost increases. Nevertheless he very consciously tried to shift blame from himself to the council and either the department heads or the unions (it was not clear which). His answers were close enough to be plausible (for example, his citation of deficits in the Police Department), but he understated the staff's responsibilities for the problem.

In the view of the assistant city manager, staff incompetence was more important. He blamed unions, but only in conjunction with the city's lack of a personnel policy, which might have avoided many disputes that eventually came up through the unions. The reason given for a lack of personnel policy was a lack of visibility of the problem, and consequently, a lack of resources devoted to personnel. He also argued that, while the city was probably somewhat overstaffed, the city manager's office had no way to evaluate departmental requests for personnel. He and the city manager had no standards of service, and were learning as they went. They needed more program and zero-based budgeting, even though the new budgeting techniques created cries of protest. The departments, he claimed, routinely padded their budgets until two years before. They now voluntarily pared down their budgets, a fact which he felt to be significant. He also criticized the city's lack of control over requisitions for largely unneeded equipment. He also argued that the city needed better inventory control and better repair services for its many new vehicles, since much money was being wasted.

The assistant city manager was less concerned with deflecting blame than most of the other informants. He was himself involved in labor negotiations and readily admitted weaknesses in this area. He asserted that the size of the deficits came as a surprise to the city. He did not come down heavily on the council, except to imply that their priorities were ordered by desire for visibility, which led them to allocate improperly. He was more concerned with the inflated requests of departments and the lack of managerial controls. He did raise the issue of low tax base, and spent time demonstrating the efforts that had been taken and could be taken to turn the situation around, lamenting the lack of incentives to attract business inside the city limits.

The assistant city manager's diagnosis was focused almost exclusively on what could be changed: the quality of personnel in key spots and the quality of budgeting procedures, control procedures, and policy. He did not invoke national trends, social trends in the city, or inflation, and he treated the low tax base not as an inevitable fact but as an element which could be affected by policy.

In short, the city staff, such as the finance director, the city manager, and the assistant manager, seemed more able to divide the blame among actors, to focus on the local situation, and to pay less attention to the importance of national social problems.

The city's employees, at least as represented by their unions, tended to blame the city administration for everything. They blamed the ineptness of a city administration that could not foresee retrenchment even a few months before it occurred. They blamed the city for not bargaining in good faith and forcing employees out on strike. They suggested that administrative ineptness was responsible for insurance increases. One union spokesman said that the city manager neglected to give council members financial impact statements, even when requested. He believed that there had been a lack of control over equipment purchases.

> The city manager opened a box of goodies, all kinds of equipment purchases simultaneous with street equipment, fire equipment, and the irony of it is that there aren't enough men to use it and it sits idle. Also, it was all bought at the same time [implying that it will all wear out at the same time]. Some of the stuff the fire chief bought was terrible quality.

A second union spokesman—this one from the police union—answered the same question in a similar way:

> The city got into fiscal trouble as a result of mismanagement. F—— was the director of finance, and J—— was the city manager. The city manager created the deficits, and then he and his budget director left. The new city manager and the new budget director were inexperienced financially, and did nothing to control the deficits. We continued to hire people, and there was too much expansion of the motorized fleet. [He later admitted that automobiles represented an insignificant portion of the deficit.] The city was split into zones for street repair. More firemen were needed

and more equipment. That was in 1975. In 1976 we laid off people. The city council is ultimately responsible, but the city manager hadn't taken action. The city manager should have informed them.

A third representative of the city's unions emphasized political favoritism more than the prior two. He suggested that the downtown banks benefited unduly from the parking deck scheme. He also mentioned that there were too many administrators and maintained that administrative ineptness led to increases in insurance rates. His analysis of the causes of fiscal stress is more interesting as a worker's view than as an explanation, since most of the events he talked of occurred much later than the onset of fiscal strain, and indeed the financial impact of the parking decks has not yet really been felt. But his overall sentiment that political favoritism caused the fiscal stress should be recorded. It was not clear whether his accusation included the city council and the city staff or only one of them.

Overall, an incredibly large number of reasons for the city's fiscal stress were offered by actors on the municipal scene. Many of them contained a kernel of truth plus a kernel of self-justification. Finding out how to combine these explanations, and what additional arguments should be included was a task in the sociology of knowledge. In order to evaluate each explanation, several criteria were used. First, could it account for the location and size of the deficits? Could it account for the timing of the deficits? Might it reasonably be used to explain the differences between cities? Is it consistent with other reports from other actors on the same subject? Is it consistent with documentary analysis? How close was the person to the actual incurrence of deficits? If he or she might have been implicated, how might this have affected the responses? Some attempt has been made in presenting the actors' arguments to show how they grouped on the basis of role in city government. What remains is to weigh the arguments listed by the actors.

Evaluation of the Actors' Explanations

Each of the actors cited a number of arguments. In this section only the key arguments will be analyzed. Some of these arguments are difficult to evaluate, and evidence may at times be indirect and inferential.

Inflation

One of the arguments cited by the former mayor is that inflation contributed to fiscal stress. The argument also appears in the introduction and explanation of the budget in 1972, in which the deficits are first acknowledged. Since inflation implies factors beyond the city's control it is important to evaluate what role it played in the generation of deficits.[1]

In analyzing the case study city, it was not possible to come up with completely accurate figures on cost inflation because of the lack of information on quantity and quality of items purchased. Nevertheless, on major items or large items for which there was adequate information, analysis was performed and the results extrapolated to the whole budget. Salary increases for employees averaged 7.9% per year from 1971 to 1977. The cost of heavy equipment, such as fire trucks, seemed to have increased at about 9.6% per year for the period from 1966 to 1974.[2] The cost of hospitalization insurance and workmen's compensation, frequently cited as rising very quickly, ran at about 6.4% increase per year per employee from 1972 to 1976 (when these increases are not controlled for number of employees, the cost increase runs at about 9.2%). By combining these increases, based on the proportion of the budget represented, and some judicious guessing, I arrived at an inflation rate for expenditures of about 8%, close to the average for cities in the state.

Estimating the impact of inflation on revenues was equally approximate due to the difficulty of separating growth from inflation. Nevertheless, some relevant summary data could be obtained. There were three major sources of locally raised revenues: property taxes, sales taxes, and water bills. Revenue from sales taxes increased at a rate of 8.5% a year from 1972 to 1976. This increase probably represented some, but not much, growth in new business, because business was generally stagnant at the time. Water and sewer revenues increased at about 7.1% a year. Since water bills are not sensitive to inflation, this increase was probably due to expansion of area served and to rate increases. The property tax revenues, by contrast with sales tax and water bills, were almost stagnant. If one examines the increase in revenues due to increase in the tax base (both real growth and inflation), without an increase in the millage rate, revenues would have increased about 2.6% a year from 1970 to 1976.

The major locally raised taxes were growing at a slower rate than inflation of expenditures. Consequently, it is correct to say that inflation contributed to the pressures toward fiscal stress. But inflation is only partly implicated, and if inflation alone had been involved, there would probably have been no deficits at all.

There are several other factors which must be kept in mind in interpreting the above results. First, there were a number of other revenue sources for the city, including intergovernmental revenues. Revenue sharing alone, which brought in over a million dollars a year, would have nearly eliminated the predicted gap between growth in revenues and growth in expenditures due to inflation. The city was also able to increase millage rates to increase revenues. Secondly, the lack of growth in property tax revenues was not simply a matter of failing to capture inflation-induced increases in the sales price of houses. There was real stagnation and even decline in the tax base. The sales value of the downtown area declined from 1972 to 1976 [1976 figures were the most recent available]. From 1970 to 1971, the assessed value of lands actually declined. From 1971 to 1972, the assessed value of lots also declined. Personal property tax assessments declined each year from 1969 to 1972, and the assessed valuation of railroads declined each year from 1966 on. The city's revenue problems reflected underlying economic and social conditions, including deteriorating housing stock, lack of municipal investment (in 1971 the city had no General Obligation Bonds outstanding), and exodus of businesses. Inflation in expenditures caused a more serious problem because of these underlying conditions; but inflation did not cause this revenue problem, nor can this problem be perceived as one imposed on the city from outside.

We have argued so far that while expenditures were affected by inflation at about 8% a year and locally raised revenues grew more slowly than inflation, additional revenue in the form of tax increases and intergovernmental revenues would have covered the gap opened by inflation. We have also argued that *the lack of growth in revenue reflected underlying economic and social conditions* and was not a problem resulting from external conditions over which the city had no control.

To put the issue of inflation in perspective, it should be remembered that the increases in expenditures each year were considerably larger than inflation and that the size of deficits was larger than the size of the gap predicted on the basis of inflation alone. There were increases in spending, for more personnel, equipment, and buildings. One of the key issues in understanding the generation of deficits has to do with why expansion took place at precisely the same time as tax revenues were flagging and expenses were increasing due to inflation.

Finally, the impact of inflation on fiscal stress was exaggerated by city officials because inflation was politically acceptable and perhaps inevitable. Sometimes officials blamed inflation when inflation did not seem to be involved. For example, the causes of deficits in 1972, listed by the city manager in that year's budget, included the following explanation:

> Because the economy has shown an increase in inflation, and because the increase in demand for city services continues to grow, the 1972 budget reflects an increase in expenditures in the following areas:

Revised cost estimate West Side Treatment plant	$3,540,850
Revised cost estimate Forest Park water and sewer	119,405
Revised cost estimate hosp. & workmen's comp	164,223
Revised cost fringe benefits, underestimated 1971	45,400
Additional costs of personnel, budgeted for 3 months in 1971	69,804
Termination of land clearance commission projects	71,000
Salary increases negotiated for 1972	284,458
New personnel in 1972	74,405

> Expenses were, therefore, 18% higher in 1972 than in 1971, while revenues increased only 16%.

In analyzing these increases, it is important to note that the proportion of the increase clearly due to inflation was small. Salary increases in the amount of $284,458 can be considered partly or wholly due to inflation, but other items are more ambiguous. The large increase in workmen's compensation and hospitalization insurance seems to have been an overestimate of expenses; two years later, with many more employees, *actual* costs were lower than the costs budgeted in 1972. The largest item was the revised cost estimate on the west side treatment plant. On detailed examination of the budget, however, this increase does not appear to be due to inflation. The federal portion of the project was budgeted at about $7,360,000, which the city seemed to expect the federal government to forward to them in 1971, for it listed that amount in expected income from the federal government and planned to expend four million dollars that year on the project. The city received only $647,400 in 1971 from the federal government. The project was postponed and the following year the city revised downward its expectation of how much the federal government would pay. The new estimate of federal revenue was $4,503,510. The city's increase was the difference between the total estimated grant and the proportion it expected to receive in 1972. The city had to come up with this amount of money in advance from local revenues. There was thus no inflation of construction costs involved in this upward revision, merely a redrawing of expectations as to the arrival of federal money. One could argue that the treatment plant itself led to increased costs and deficits, or that inexperience with federal grants led to the deficits. But the cause was not primarily inflation.

To summarize, inflation had some impact on expenditures, but much more of the expenditure increase was due to expansion rather than to increase in cost of items formerly purchased. This was as true in equipment as in personnel. The real cost increases resulted from addition of equipment, expansion of the Police, Fire, and Street Departments, and increased salaries and benefits. New hiring continued up to the period of multimillion dollar deficits in 1975. With some natural growth in tax base and inflation-sensitive sales tax revenues, combined with revenue sharing funds, the city could have come close to meeting all its obligations at former service levels. Inflation complicated the financial picture and made recovery more difficult. Fiscal stress was made more serious by the lack of real growth in the tax base, a separate problem from inflation.

Lack of Investment and Growth

The city manager pointed to a prior pattern of lack of investment, followed by a decision to get the city moving again. Initial attempts to develop the city were clumsy, but such attempts were gradually becoming more successful. The city manager also argued that the city had grown in population and in area and now had to cope with that growth.

This set of arguments is accurate as far as corroborating data is concerned. It accounts for the timing of fiscal stress as well as the manner in which it occurred, and for the location of deficits in the various funds.

The city's population and areal growth had been severely undercapitalized. In the early 1970s, the city had no outstanding general obligation debt. Construction costs for police and fire stations were frequently paid for by conventional bank loans then repaid from current revenues in the operating budget. The only long-term debt outstanding was that of the Water and Sewer Department, and it was self-liquidating.

After 1972, the increased area of the city and new construction led to new capital outlay and higher operating costs in Fire, Streets, and Water and Sewer. The Water and Sewer Department built and staffed a new sewage disposal plant to cope with the population expansion in the newer areas of the city. The Fire Department relocated two stations and built two new stations to cope with the changing patterns of residential settlement. The new stations necessitated land acquisition, construction costs, furnishing and operating costs, new equipment, and more men. The Street Department was involved with repair in the downtown and putting in streets in the new shopping mall. More new equipment was purchased, and some new employees were hired. Areal expansion per se did not explain the increases in the costs of police, however.

Crime, Civil Unrest, and Police Costs

The former mayor attributed the enormous expansion in the Police Department to crime rates and civil disorder. I interpreted his comments to mean that fear of crime in general and fear of blacks especially, triggered an increase in demand for police. The civil unrest of which he spoke occurred after Martin Luther King's death. It was just after the riots that the first large increase in police manpower took place. Councilmen talked freely in the 1960s (and were quoted in the newspapers) of wanting to increase the size of the department "because people they knew had been jumped just outside the downtown" (in the black neighborhoods). The rest of the data supported the former mayor's argument. Fear of crime, racial riots, and racial antagonism more broadly viewed created demand for more police. This demand was reflected in councilmanic support of police expansion, both publicly at council meetings, and privately at budget sessions. The councilmen's requests that police be highly visible reflected the need for making people feel secure and protected. The resulting pressure, when combined with professional desires for police expansion coming from within the department, led to the increased police expenditures noted above. Combined with political unwillingness to raise taxes for these additional services and the lack of real growth in the city to generate new revenues, the increase in police services was a major contributor to deficits.

Outsiders

A number of causes of fiscal stress can be grouped under the label "outsiders." That is, several informants blamed outsiders or national trends as the cause of their problems. The politicians, in particular, were prone to this type of explanation. Many of these explanations are partly true.

For example, union militance was attributed both to outsiders and to national trends. It was true that the local unions had the help of statewide union support, and it was a militant organizer from outside who finally took the fire union out on strike. It is also true, to an extent, that the unionization and activation of public sector employees imitated private sector labor. But the city's unions also had a long list of internal grievances, including a change from a lax fire chief to a strict disciplinarian, whose punishments were seen as either arbitrary or antiunion; several years with low or no salary increases, due to fiscal crisis; attempts by the city manager to weaken the unions; and an inept administration which let the deficits happen and then took it out on the unions. The unions had a legitimate complaint that the city had put the salary settlement in the budget without bargaining. There were thus a number of complaints against local conditions, which might not alone have precipitated a strike but when combined with outside expertise, resulted in strike action.

A second argument for the influence of outsiders is in the city's race riots. Newspaper clippings in the former mayor's files suggested that local racial unrest was imitative of civil rights demonstrations elsewhere rather than rooted in local conditions. The former mayor argued in his interview that rioters to whom he spoke were drunken outsiders. Race relations in the city had always been good, he claimed, and they had never expected riots. While conditions for blacks may not have been as bad in Southside as elsewhere, the high level of prejudice and social tension was reflected in the kind of issues over which conflict took place. They included courtesy in downtown stores and social acceptance in the public schools. Quarrels broke out over whether or not there should be a black prom queen or a black cheerleader. Living conditions in black areas were poor, and relations between police and blacks were terrible. The year after the riots the Police Department commissioned a study on how to improve those relationships. The first half of the report documented the extent of the disaffection. The second half recommended sensitivity training for police. In short, while outside influences were present, there were also internal conditions underlying events.

The third kind of argument about outsiders was that the state and/or the federal government was responsible for fiscal stress. Respondents argued in terms of the impact of the overall tax bite and of state budgeting requirements for earmarked funds. The former mayor, in particular, argued that other governmental units were more wasteful than the cities and that because citizens had to pay so much in other taxes, they were reluctant to pay increased taxes to the city. There was some plausibility to this argument, but it hardly justified the waste or corruption in the city. The overall tax burden probably did aggravate voter reluctance to pay additional taxes and this provided an outside impact on fiscal stress, since politicians, seeing the overall tax burden as a restraint on city revenues, did not raise taxes when expenses increased.

The argument that state regulations over budgeting caused the fiscal crisis was untrue. If anything, state regulations were too laxly enforced. The city was underfunding its pension funds. Enforcement of state statutes showed up city practices. In the case of pension funds, however, it is true that being forced to pay back money not paid into the funds further strained the budget.

The politicians concentrated on outside agitators and the state and federal governments as causes of fiscal stress. When the staff blamed outsiders, it was a more immediate set of outsiders with more concrete impact on the budget. The city manager, for example, blamed the county, a local judge, and an arbitrator for decisions that went against the city. The county collected property taxes for all the jurisdictions inside it and, by holding back the revenue to earn interest on it, forced the city to borrow until the county released the funds. The county treasurer, admitting that this practice occurred, claimed the county did not want to begin short-term borrowing to cover its revenue problems. Financial problems at the county level thus exacerbated financial problems at the city level, increasing interest payments, and creating cash flow problems, and adding to uncertainty. The local judge became involved when the city manager sought an injunction against striking firemen. The judge forced the two parties to negotiate and allowed the strike to continue a week. The final settlement was larger than the city's budgeted amount for salary increase. More expensive was the arbitrator's settlement when a dispute about membership in the union by officers (as opposed to rank and file) ended up in a salary dispute about the differential pay for officers and men, first in the police, and then in the fire union. The arbitrator paid no attention to the city's financial problems, and awarded an overall 18% increase. Outsiders in these cases did indeed affect the city's finances in a negative way and contributed to deficits by increasing expenditures. The union settlement, in particular, had cumulative effects.

Outsiders did play a substantial role in causing financial stress. Sometimes by operating in the background, they set up a pattern for expression of discontent. At other times they were the immediate cause of problems, with the underlying causes inside the city. In most cases, it was a combination of internal and external actors and influences that made the impact on finances. Politicians' assertions that it was only outsiders that caused fiscal stress were not sustained by the data.

Expansion of Scope: Increased Demands without a Willingness to Pay

The politicians also argued that the cause of fiscal stress was that citizens wanted more services than in the past but were unwilling to pay for them. One politician argued that the *society* had created a dependency on government through welfare programs. People expected the government to do things for them. The former mayor argued that the scope of services had increased.

These arguments did not stand up well as independent causes of fiscal stress. Southside did not enlarge its governmental scope during the period of buildup of fiscal stress. While playing an increased role in housing and transportation, the city did not pay for these activities out of the budget. They could not have caused the deficits.

Secondly, the fact that all or most people wanted services without paying for them does not necessitate fiscal stress. Presumably people everywhere want something for nothing; they do not therefore get it. If politicians feel that the way to get votes is to give people services without appearing to pay for them, it is as much the politicians' actions as the people's desires which are to blame. The argument that people are unwilling to pay for services they demand is not a particularly convincing explanation of fiscal stress. This is especially so since popular desires must be expressed through the political system and must be controlled and responded to by city staff and the council. The political and administrative machinery is supposed to restrict service outputs to what revenues can purchase. Demands are not automatically translated into outputs, as suggested in the politicians' model.

Managerial Ineptness

Several informants charged fiscal stress to administrative ineptness. It can be difficult in practice to separate weakness from ineptness, but the actors themselves suggested that inexperience of key staff contributed to deficits. The handling or mishandling of grant revenues appeared to contribute directly to deficits. The city manager admitted that he and his budget officer both were inexperienced in 1972. The assistant city manager indicated a lack of standards by which to evaluate the required amount of equipment. It is also difficult to question the union negotiatior's charge that only an inept city staff would not be able to foresee major layoffs three months before they took place. The staff seemed constantly surprised by the size of deficits and later, just before the strike, indicated that the unions would not strike. City staff always seemed to be caught off balance. Other informants charged that the city manager did not provide financial impact assessments for annexations even when councilmembers requested them. Another charge was that the city manager should have warned the council about the deficits before they became so large. Whatever the truth in these charges, it is clear that inexperience in key positions helped to permit or facilitated the changes that led to fiscal stress.

The Unions

City staff often blamed the unions for unsettling wage agreements,[3] but it is clear from the case study that the unions were only partly responsible for the large settlements. Moreover, there were several moderate or lean years for each year of generous settlement. The timing of labor negotiations during the budget process gave the appearance that labor settlements caused the deficits, but had they come earlier, then the special projects or equipment requests would either have had to be cut or would have caused the deficits.

The unions had little effect on staffing levels, which were written into "manning clauses" (how many men per station, of what rank, how many men per truck, or car, and so forth), and primarily determined by the chief. The firemen argued that the greater the number of men on the truck, the greater the safety, and would have liked higher numbers than the city could afford. At the time of the study, however, manning clauses were beyond the scope of negotiable issues. The drive for expansion in the Fire Department came from the chief as he strove to improve the city's fire rating as a measure of his professional skills. The unions cannot be scored on this account.

While manning clauses were not negotiated, many "management prerogatives" were eroded by the labor contract. The police chief, in particular, complained that the resulting rigidity prevented economizing when cutbacks became necessary. He claimed that such managerial prerogatives were being eroded in the Fire Department. While the fire chief denied this assertion, the contract itself supported the police chief. The items involved rules for the assignment of personnel, promotion of the most senior employees by lot, and specifications on the quality of socks and teeshirts purchased as a benefit to employees.

The immediate costs of such rigidity were not felt in dollars but in the quality of service, since the possibility of promotion for merit was eliminated along with promotion on the basis of favoritism. The contract set up for the future a situation in which more and more men will be required to do the same amount of work (declining productivity) and will make future cutbacks more difficult. But such rigidity was not the cause of the deficits of the 1970s.

As indicated by the former mayor, the major role played by the unions in the deficits themselves was in gaining benefits after recognition in 1969. The unions gained at that time a large increase in benefits, which became continually more expensive as time went on. The unions, incidentally, did not ask for education benefits. The rank and file felt that it was not fair for a few men to get higher salary increases than the others. Education benefits were thrown in as an incentive by management (*professional* staff), but the unions almost gave them back under pressure from the rank and file. Later they became very expensive, and the city had to trade other benefits to get them back.

Secondly, the unions insured that the city had to increase salaries at least as much as the cost of living. This prevented the city from countering inflation by reducing the purchasing power of employees.

Despite the importance of increased benefits and salary settlements, the politicians were probably correct when they questioned the interviewer's characterization of the unions as militant. The unions were moderately passive. As the police union spokesman put it,

We have been well paid [due to professionalism of the department head]; we don't feel militant about salaries. We have a good chief whom we can talk out grievances with, and we are structually weak because there are so many alternative police agencies to step in if we go out on strike.

The militance of the unions, such as it was, was built up in the several years in which the city was trying to cut down expenses. It was the fiscal crisis which prompted the city manager to try to weaken the unions, which infuriated them. It was the fiscal crisis which prompted layoffs of new recruits several months after they had moved to the city to comply with residency requirements. It was the fiscal crisis which reduced salary increases. Real union militance, in short, was a product of the fiscal crisis rather than a cause.

Patronage and Overstaffing

The city finance officer suggested that the Police Department was overstaffed. While this was probably true, patronage hiring was not a major source of fiscal stress. Every few years, there seemed to be a revival of summer hiring of teenagers to cut weeds on vacant lots, but the total cost was low. Employees, as well as staff and politicians, all agreed that hiring was fairly straightforward and honest. If a politically recommended candidate was otherwise qualified, then the support of the department head would be useful, but demonstrated competence was the major staff concern. To the extent that the city's financial problems were caused by overstaffing, they were probably not the result of patronage appointments.

The kind of overstaffing the budget officer cited was too many highly paid assistants to the chief (staffers) and too many highly paid technicians, such as electricians. This kind of overstaffing probably reflected the aspiration for professionalism by the chief and patrolmen. It provided white collar desk jobs in a department where the opportunities for promotion were limited and where work hours for blue collar jobs were often disruptive to family and social life.

One union spokesman suggested that corruption was involved in generating fiscal stress. How much corruption there was on construction and on purchases of goods and services is impossible to ascertain. Council members claimed in interviews that there was little or no such corruption because on bids the council was under the control of the city manager. Yet they accused each other of letting bids to favorite companies and of not accepting the lowest bidder. The bidding process had fallen into such chaos that frequently there were no bidders or only one bid, because potential bidders did not believe the bidding was honest. In this case, mere belief in the existence of corruption probably had almost as much financial impact as corruption itself, since it thwarted competitive bidding. Charges of corruption in the construction of the parking decks were also impossible to pin down. It seemed unlikely, however, that individuals pocketed large sums of money. More likely, the project was the result of active interest group politics and the deteriorating tax base. The banks especially, with their extensive investments in the downtown, had an interest in rebuilding it. Reserving space in the parking decks for bank employees, alluded to as evidence of corruption, was minor. The assignment of parking spaces may have represented a deal the city made with the banks to encourage them to construct new buildings downtown (which they did), but this arrangement did not generate the deficits.

Causes of Fiscal Stress: Interactions over Time

Respondents identified a number of causes of fiscal stress which met the standards of evidence: they were corroborated by quantitative data, they helped account for the timing and pattern of occurrence of deficits, and they provided a basis for comparison with other cities. But the actors did not put the causes of fiscal stress in historical sequence, nor did they show how various factors interacted over time. Therefore this section will offer a historical version of the development of fiscal stress. The process of getting into and out of fiscal stress will be divided into stages: predisposing factors, precipitating events, prolonging factors, and correcting mechanisms.

Predisposing Factors

Many characteristics of the city were well-developed decades before the onset of fiscal stress. This study contends that changes in major areas of economy, politics, and social life precipitated the fiscal crisis and influenced the timing and manner of its occurrence.

The first was a change in the economic base of the city. The city's dependence on only one or two industries made it perhaps more vulnerable to fiscal stress. Gradually, over the course of thirty or forty years, the steel mills declined and petrochemicals became the dominant industry. The closing of a federal facility in the late 1960s began an out-migration of a stable middle-class group of residents. Following the federal facility, several other major employers left the city.

The second major change was the in-migration of blacks (and later, Hispanics) throughout the 1950s, 1960s and 1970s. Slower hiring in the steel mills and economic stagnation combined with the lower average educational levels of the migrants and with the prejudices of earlier residents to prevent blacks from getting good jobs. Lower average family incomes contributed to the concentration of blacks in older rental units in the city's east side. High density, poverty, fires, crime, prejudice, and disinvestment contributed to a spreading slum.

As conditions worsened in the black ghettos, the impetus to suburbanization was fed by fear of crime, fear of blacks, and accelerating decay of housing and basic services. By the early 1970s, there was a steady exodus of whites to the outskirts of the city. When the city stopped annexing residential neighborhoods, this pattern stood out clearly. In the mid-seventies, total population began to decline, and the percentage of blacks and Hispanics increased rapidly. The basic pattern involved several stages: influx of blacks, ghettoization and the creation of slum conditions, white exodus, annexation of suburbs, cessation of annexations of residential neighborhoods, and population decline.

The social changes associated with in-migration of blacks had far-reaching financial impacts on the city. The location of the poor black and Hispanic neighborhoods around the downtown area, combined with the exodus of the more prosperous residents to newer west side neighborhoods, did much to weaken the downtown and create a new economic center of gravity. During the 1970s, the decline of the sales value of downtown properties affected the growth of revenues, and helped prompt efforts to regenerate the downtown. Also, the annexation of new (white) subdivisions contributed to doubling the city's area between 1970 and 1978. The increase in area contributed to increases in cost of services not compensated by revenues.

The third set of predisposing events were changes in the political structure of the city. The city gradually changed from a strong-mayor form in 1955 to a real city manager form in the early 1970s. During the period of transition there was considerable patronage, nepotism, and some scandal. Salaries for municipal workers were low, and turnover was high. There were municipal unions but no collective bargaining. By the mid-1960s, performance of municipal services had become problematic. More water was lost through leaks than was metered, and scandals in the Police Department resulted in the chief's firing and in attempts to redesign the department along more professional lines. The tide was turning toward professionalism and expertise and away from political loyalty and favors. Over the same period of time, bloc voting had deteriorated, partly as the result of at-large nonpartisan elections, but also partly through social changes that made it less acceptable for some people to tell others how to vote. The machine was losing its grip. By 1972 it was possible for the city manager to fire political appointees unqualified for their jobs.

The long and gradual shift from strong-mayor, machine-style politics to city manager reform-style politics had many consequences that contributed to fiscal stress. First, even in 1972, the city manager was in a structurally weak position. He was working with a council split

between reformed and unreformed members, which curtailed his ability to cut budgets. Also, he had a small staff and was unable to carry
out some portions of financial control normally associated with reformed government. Secondly, the gradual elimination of most patronage and of voting blocs left politicians vulnerable to the demands
of any group of organized voters. The municipal unions were the key
group which could swing large numbers of votes, and they became
increasingly important as the city became more reformed. The councilmen's unwillingness to make labor policy reflected this vulnerability
and resulted in expensive labor settlements. To relate the inability of
the city manager to cut budget requests with the decline of patronage,
one should recall that the city manager's refusal to grant patronage
positions to unqualified applicants antagonized council members,
making the city manager fear for his job. Because of this, he could not
press his attempts to cut special projects of councilmen from the
budget.

One of the few successes of the reformed government was increased
professionalism. But professionalism itself generated expenses. Professionalism implies an image of a good water system or a good Police
Department, which involves staffing levels, technical goals, quality
equipment, and trained professional staff. Achieving such ideals can
be extraordinarily expensive.

To reiterate, there were three major sets of changes that created
predispositions to fiscal stress: economic, social and political. These
changes had continuing effects into the 1970s when the deficits first
occurred, effects that were sharpened by conditions just prior to and
during the early phases of fiscal stress.

Precipitating Events

Precipitating events, like the underlying causes, also included economic, social and political elements. Economic events included inflation on the one hand and a tapering off of assessed valuations on the
other. Socially, there were racial confrontations. Politically there was
a response to the riots and to the first deficits, as well as an apparent
change in budgeting practices.

The city was squeezed by an inflation rate in goods and services of
around 8% and increases in local revenues that lagged somewhat behind this rate. The lack of growth in assessed valuations was the combined effect of neglect of the downtown, changing social composition,
loss of some taxes, and the continuing decline of the importance of
railroads to the city's economy. The stagnation in assessed values at

the same time as a slowdown in revenue growth from sales taxes caused considerably less growth in revenue than the city would normally expect.

The reaction of political leaders at the time the first deficits appeared was less constructive than it might have been. In 1971 they actually lowered the millage rates in some areas, although there had been no decline in expenditures. They showed extreme reluctance to raise tax rates to compensate for the leveling out of revenues. The strategy for handling deficits outlined in the 1972 budget was to hold down new hires and try to generate additional revenue or even find new sources of revenue. Revenue growth was a more politically acceptable solution, but it was a much slower process than raising tax rates.

To complicate matters, the new city manager who took over in 1972 announced a policy of bringing the department heads and the city council closer together. He provided many opportunities for them to do so. The result was an alliance between department heads and the council that raised the budget requests of the departments while protecting them from being cut by the city manager.

The precipitating event in the social realm was the racial riots of 1968. The city's reaction to the riots was to smooth over the problems, calm them down, and handle as many of the resulting demands as it could. The city's reaction was twofold: on the one hand it created a new office of community relations to deal with problems such as discrimination in jobs and housing, and on the other hand, it greatly expanded and improved the Police Department. The riots provided the impetus to continue to implement the police reforms begun in 1966. Of the two strategies, the cost of expanding the Police Department was much greater than the cost of the new Community Relations Office.

The riots had an indirect effect on labor relations at city hall as well as a direct effect on the costs of police expenditures. First, they created a new sense of solidarity among firemen who worked together long hours during the riots. Second, the fact that firemen were attacked during the riots startled them out of their self-image as heroes. Like the policemen who were viewed by portions of the public as "pigs," the firemen suffered a status degradation that lent impetus to union militancy. The danger faced by uniformed services during the riots was used as a reason for negotiated contracts and for more liberal benefits, especially insurance. It was at this time that unions won the right to bargain collectively and gained substantial benefits. Finally, the increase in the number of policemen, which was the first major impact of the riots, increased the union's voting power on one hand and increased the costs of negotiated benefits on the other.

Given the context of predisposing and precipitating factors, it is perhaps not difficult to see how the city fell into deficit spending. It is more problematic to analyze why the deficits continued to grow from 1971 to 1976. A variety of factors prolonged the crisis besides the lagged effects of prior events.

Prolonging Factors

The factors which prolonged the deficits can also be grouped as social, economic and political:

Socially, the out-migration of whites to new subdivisions, which was followed by annexations, created a new, more intense racial and economic segregation in the city. This spacial segregation contributed to political opposition to downtown renewal from the newer, wealthier portions of the city. The ensuing political battle slowed the downtown development. Also, the delayed effects of areal expansion crept into the budget as higher service and capital costs.

Economically, the efforts to increase the tax base actually prolonged the deficits. As early as 1972, when the revenue problem was first recognized, the city manager recommended efforts to increase the tax base. By 1973, arrangements were made for the shopping mall. These arrangements demanded high capital investments for the city and increased operating costs. The shopping mall would not bring in much revenue for several more years. Moreover, the completion of the mall depleted the downtown businesses and thus accelerated the need for preserving that area. A second project was then begun to restore the downtown. These large projects, at a time when the city was hard pressed financially, required heavy outlays before they returned any revenue. Moreover, the shopping mall dramatically increased the city's area and hence the costs of ordinary services.

Two political problems prolonged the crisis. First was the attempt to hide and thereby minimize the deficits. Then, once their size was known, the strategy of controlling costs by breaking the unions backfired.

In the early years the deficits were hidden entirely. Later a number of techniques were used to minimize the size of deficits. This minimizing of deficits undoubtedly contributed to the lack of energy exercised in eliminating them. Once their size was established and acknowledged, they were still too large to cut back all at once and too large to cover with a jump in tax rates without jeopardizing the job of the city manager. The inability to eliminate deficits resulted at least in part from the weakness of the city manager with respect to the council and his fear of getting fired.

The second political factor prolonging the deficits was the city manager's attempt to weaken the unions. Unable to cut projects that councilmen and department heads agreed on, he turned to the unions as a possible source of savings. His attempts to weaken the unions were seen as "union busting" and angered union leaders. The ensuing battle resulted in binding arbitration that was very expensive for the city. Later attempts to dictate salary increases rather than negotiate them also angered the unions and brought on strike action and a more expensive settlement.

Correcting Mechanisms

What finally brought the crisis to an end? The first element in provoking a turnaround was the decline in assessed valuations. By 1972 the city manager seemed to be aware of the problem of declining assessments, and others became aware of it in the next few years. A drop in the rate of revenue growth prompted attempts to regenerate the tax base. A councilman in 1976 insisted that efforts to increase the tax base were not related to deficits so much as to stagnation of the tax base. To carry out the financial aspects of redevelopment, the finance director had to be fired and replaced by his predecessor.

When the "new" finance director took over, he reorganized the budget to show the councilmen the extent of deficits. A second corrective mechanism was thereby brought into play: the visibility of the deficits prompted tax increases.

A third corrective mechanism was set into motion by the need for a better bond rating in order to execute the shopping center project. It was in an effort to improve the city's bond rating that many of the most dramatic changes, including the cutbacks of 1976, were undertaken. At that time the city's planning department concluded from a study of the causes of the financial problems that unwise annexations of residential property were partly at fault, as well as the overall low assessed valuation. The council then adopted a more conservative policy toward annexations. Finally, after years of publicly acknowledged deficits, a poor bond rating, and labor troubles, the city manager was replaced by a stronger, more experienced administrator. The new city manager restructured the budget process to break up the alliance between the department heads and the council.

Ironically, not the deficits themselves but the slowdown in growth of revenues triggered recovery. The growth in revenues had provided discretionary funds for salary increases and special projects, of particular concern to councilmen. As soon as they understood that there was no slack, they strove to re-create the growth. Unless large and embarrassing, deficits were not of immediate concern. The effort to rebuild the tax base publicized the size and extent of deficits enough to motivate official action to eliminate them.

Seven

The Fiscal Crisis:
A Self-Correcting City?

By 1978, Southside had eliminated at least the planned deficits and perhaps the actual ones as well. It did so without bankruptcy and without substantial reorganization of its debt. One can think of this as a self-correcting, equilibrating process. But did Southside really heal itself? What was the role of outsiders in solving the city's fiscal crisis? Did the city really merely postpone fiscal collapse rather than solve its financial problems?

Outside Agents and Fiscal Change

Three outside actors played a major role in the city's recovery: Moody's and the state and federal governments. Since there was no sweeping rescue of the city by emergency loans or reorganization of debt, none of these actors played a totally unambiguous role. This section attempts to weigh the overall impact of each external actor.

Moody's

The role of Moody's is the clearest and simplest. By revising the city's credit rating downward, Moody's in one stroke made the city's financial plight public and increased the cost of borrowing for the city. Moreover, Moody's kept up constant pressure on the city by threatening either to lower the rating still further or to withdraw it entirely unless *major* improvements were made. Moody's bond rating prompted the city to make its cutbacks in 1976 and to reduce the deficits to zero in such a relatively short time. Despite the financial impact of increased costs of borrowing, the overall effect of Moody's was beneficial to the city. It was the basis for many of the internal changes which took place.

State Government

The state government played a slightly more complicated but also benevolent role. Through a program of equalizing assessed valuations, the state forced up the assessment-sales ratio in the city, which increased the assessed valuation even where sales value was stagnant or declining. As a result, revenues were sustained when they might have declined. When the city increased its tax rate, the effect in increased revenues was multiplied because of the concurrent increase in assessment-sales ratio. The state thus created windfall revenues for the city at a time when they were desperately needed. But the increase generated in this manner is temporary. Once the assessment-sales ratio reaches a particular fixed level, it will cease to rise. After that time, any drop in sales value will show up in revenue losses. Moreover, the revenue increase derived in this manner was a mixed blessing, since it substantially increased the assessments of a number of citizens simultaneously with increases in property tax *rates*. There is a limit to how much additional property tax people will pay. After that limit is reached, contested payments and tax delinquencies increase. Since contested payments are impounded by the county and held until adjudication, the city might not get its revenue for years. Moreover, the proportion of the city's tax levy which it would receive any given year would become unpredictable.

A second impact of the state on the local fiscal crisis came from its insistence that the city pay a larger amount of money into its pension funds. This requirement necessitated high short-term costs at a time when the city was finding it difficult to raise adequate revenues. In the long term, however, this outside pressure will result in sounder pension funds and avoid even more serious trouble. It will also curb the tendency to give unions pension benefits rather than salary, sometimes a tempting way of borrowing from the future and avoiding current outlay.

Federal Government

The role of the federal government was less easily determined because of the number of different kinds of programs received by the city and because of the lack of clear relationships between federal grants and fiscal stress. In order to evaluate the impact of the federal role in solving the city's financial problems, a crude balance sheet was devised which listed the problems involved in federal grants and the benefits obtained. The city's particular package of aid was then analyzed in terms of this list of effects, and attempts were made to estimate the magnitude of the effect. The list of benefits included reducing deficits, reducing bonded indebtedness, encouraging and facilitating necessary projects, and solving long-term underlying problems. The list of costs included entailed expenditures; expenditures on projects of low priority which would not otherwise be made; increased vulnerability to future fluctuations in revenue; and increased managerial difficulties, such as difficulty in predicting revenues, maintaining restricted accounts, and so on.[1]

The city received federal aid from a number of sources, but the most important were revenue sharing, HUD block grants, CETA, and the EPA. As a group, their impact began in 1972, concomitant with the beginning of fiscal stress. The city had received little federal aid in the 1960s. It had participated in neither federal urban renewal nor model cities. The timing of federal aid was important and invited a detailed investigation of the linkages between federal aid and fiscal problems.

Revenue Sharing

Revenue sharing funds were the first federal funds to make a major impact on the city. They appeared as windfall revenues of approximately one million dollars a year, with no commensurate obligations for expenditures, and no elaborate mechanics of application, reporting, accounting, and the like. The city was able to estimate the amounts involved with a fair degree of accuracy and the funds arrived within the fiscal year. This program appeared designed to solve the city's fiscal crisis by eliminating deficits. The funds were spent primarily on public safety and secondarily on community agencies engaged in helping the poor, the sick, and the elderly. When the fiscal crisis became known, the money was spent entirely to reduce the Fire Department's deficits. The money was flexible, that is, not restricted to any account, which made it particularly attractive for eliminating deficits in funds that were not receiving enough property tax. The money was also used to pay regular wages. In 1978, the city manager acknowledged that using these funds for salaries was dangerous since revenue sharing could be eliminated. On the other hand, he insisted that the city could not eliminate the practice while also eliminating the deficits.

Revenue sharing thus played a complicated role in the city. Initially, it provided some revenue for quasi-public functions not performed within the scope of city government. Then it helped reduce the size of deficits, at the same time that it enabled the city to augment its personnel beyond what local revenues could support. The expansion of personnel in 1975, which enlarged the deficits, may be partly attributed to this source: federal funds made additional employees seem cheaper than they were. Finally, at the end of 1978, the city was extremely vulnerable to changes in the structure of federal funding. A decline or elimination of funding for revenue sharing or a change in the formula for funding would cause an automatic deficit and possible cutbacks.

The city received additional funds in the revenue sharing program as countercyclical funds to offset negative economic conditions in 1977 and 1978. These funds, amounting to about two hundred thousand dollars each year, were budgeted entirely to the Police Department to reduce deficits, only a small portion of which were thus eliminated.

HUD Block Grant

The next major grant program was the HUD block grant. The city made the necessary application for this grant in 1973. Money did not arrive until 1976. Unlike revenue sharing this grant entailed considerable administrative work, including the grant application, reports, and a separate audit. It was entirely federally funded, however, which was attractive to the city; there were no entailed costs. It allowed the city to shift substantial portions of the cost of development away from local onto federal revenues. In 1978, the Community Relations Office was also shifted into the grant. The pressure from deficits in the general fund was thus alleviated somewhat.

The programmatic focus of the grant was to shore up marginal neighborhoods, to repair streets and improve drainage, fix houses, keep them occupied, and keep neighborhoods stable. The program seemed moderately successful in reducing the number of vacant houses and stabilizing neighborhoods. Citizens took an active role in deciding on improvements. Unlike the revenue sharing hearings, public input helped to determine the choice of projects. The fact that the government was paying any attention at all to these neighborhoods was encouraging to the residents.

The HUD block grant was unique in that it tried to solve one of the basic problems underlying the fiscal crisis—neighborhood deterioration and flight to the suburbs. The program was well-conceived, well-staffed, and well-administered. Its major difficulty was that its small scope prevented it from making much impact on the immediate problem of the declining east side.[2]

EPA

The third major source of federal funding was the EPA. In 1972 the city built a sewage treatment plant on the west side to accommodate the new growth in that portion of the city. The expenditure, a lagged effect of areal growth, reflected population flight followed by annexation. Capital expenditure had been delayed until 1972 when the city floated a bond to pay for the sewage treatment plant. The federal and state governments both paid for substantial portions of the total cost, but the money did not arrive until several years later. The city's share of the capital outlay was 25%, which was covered by the bond. Of more immediate financial impact, however, was the entailed expense of increased manpower and maintenance, and the difficulty of maintaining geographically dispersed plants. According to the director of the Sewer and Water Department, the default in the operating fund of the Water and Sewer Department in 1975 was partly related to this increase in operating costs.

The EPA also underwrote the city's geographical expansion to incorporate the new shopping center. In 1978, about three and a half million dollars were added to the city's federal revenues to reimburse it for sewer and water projects related to the development.

The EPA mandated the separation of storm water and sewage systems. The initial study, the planning, and the project itself would be underwritten in part by the EPA and in part by the city. This expense was pending but had not yet been incurred at the time of the field work. The project was illustrative, however, of EPA pressure on the city to make improvements in water and sewage treatment and of the entailed costs involved for the city.

CETA

The fourth major federal program to impact on the city during the 1970s was CETA. CETA funds paid the city to hire citizens who had been unemployed and/or needed training. For the cost of training, which was not out-of-pocket expense, the city could get additional staff. There were no entailed costs. CETA was used to rehire personnel who had been laid off during the cuts in 1976. Rehiring of laid-off personnel was not the purpose of CETA grants; consequently CETA administrators cited the city for abuses.

To summarize, federal funds, of such little local significance in the 1960s, played a role in every stage of fiscal stress. Federal programs helped force the city to make capital improvements that had been neglected during growth. They also helped to stabilize and rebuild neighborhoods and allowed the city expand in a way that could bring new revenues. Federal programs helped to reduce both borrowing and the size of deficits and helped to minimize the impact of budgetary cutbacks.

On the negative side, federal programs introduced a new complexity to budgeting. They increased vulnerability to future fluctuations in revenue because grants were used for salaries in basic services. They encouraged the addition of personnel by obscuring their real costs. Finally, they sometimes required matching or other costs which contributed to fiscal stress. But federal grants should not be blamed exclusively for the continued personnel expansion of the 1970s. The city's problems with overstaffing began before the federal grants and were deeply rooted in the political system and in social cleavages.

On balance, the role of the federal government was positive. Nevertheless, the efforts of both the federal government and the state combined did not solve the fiscal crisis. To the extent that the city's financial problems were either superficial, externally caused, or temporary, then infusions of unrestricted funds such as revenue sharing could be of real use. To the extent that deeper internal problems could be solved with large amounts of money, then federal and state earmarked money could also solve problems. Southside's financial problems had resulted from a prior lack of investment, physical decay, out-migration, annexation, and the political relationship between the council and the department heads. Short-term infusions of revenue—or even long-term increases in revenue with no programmatic focus—decreased the size of deficits but brought about no changes. The patterns which brought about the deficits were still operative.

The program-oriented grants, EPA and HUD, came closer to solving real underlying problems dependent on capital investments. EPA and HUD both bypassed the council's reluctance to spend for large projects or to accept federal monies with their attendant strings. The EPA forced the city to take action under the Federal Water Pollution Control Act. HUD lured the city with a 100% federally funded program. The HUD program was probably too small to make a major impact. Other major problems besides the stabilization of neighborhoods, such as the need to stabilize businesses, threatened to overshadow the small projects of the HUD grant.

Internal Changes

If the state and federal government did not bail the city out, can we conclude that with state and federal help the city bailed itself out? What kind of changes occurred in the city prior to the elimination of deficits? Were these changes of a sort likely to affect the long-run fiscal integrity of the city? Or was there merely a belt tightening? Was the burden of increased taxation pushed onto the taxpayer without reforms, making a recurrence of fiscal stress likely within the context of a higher tax effort and less financial flexibility?

Economic Redevelopment Efforts

The city could not do much about inflation, except perhaps to curb expenditures, which it tried to do from 1976 onward. But the physical decay of the city and the loss of businesses was at least partly controllable, and the city tried to stem the downward trend. The annexation of land for the new shopping mall represented a major attempt to keep businesses within the city and to increase sales and property taxes. The city also engaged in downtown renewal to restore property values and reverse the physical deterioration around the downtown area. As part of that effort, the city entered into negotiations with the banks to encourage private renewal of buildings. The idea behind such private renewal was not only to make the area more attractive but also to use banking as the core of a new growth industry dependent on face-to-face communications.

It is not yet clear if the new shopping mall will generate development around it or if there are already too many malls in the area. Nor is it clear if the new mall will generate enough increased revenues in time to pay off the bonded debt the city acquired to develop the land on which the mall is built. The city may experience another budget crunch when it comes time to begin paying debt service on this project. If the shopping mall on the edge of town was a risky project for the city, the downtown redevelopment is even more risky. It is not at all clear that the downtown mall and shopping decks can restore the viability of the downtown. Though lovely to look at, the mall and the decks do not solve the basic problem that the downtown is surrounded by the poor: poor whites, poor blacks and poor Hispanics. Nor does the downtown project necessarily solve the problem of businesses moving to follow their middle-class customers to the new subdivisions.

Social Cleavages

The tensions that generated the riots in the 1960s have abated some-what, but the hatred between the blacks and the police is still strong and liable to flare up over individual incidents. Whites' fears of blacks are still strong, and the out-migration from the city has shown no sign of abatement during the 1970s. This continued racial antipathy makes residential stability difficult and has contributed to the net population decline apparent since the mid-1970s. Other than the HUD block grant, the city has taken no major steps to stabilize neighborhoods or to reduce racial tension. The Community Relations Office, created after the riots, is still a weak influence on city government.

Political Restructuring

In theory, political problems are more manipulable than economic base erosion or racial antagonism. The three political problems em-phasized in previous chapters as causes of fiscal stress are (1) the weak political base of councilmen and the consequent strength of interest groups, especially the unions; (2) the effects of the city man-ager's weakness and the alliance between council members and depart-ments heads; and (3) the effects of council norms, values, and re-sources. Each of these political problems will be explored in turn, to see if any change occurred, and if so, whether it was temporary or cyclical in nature or if it seemed permanent.

Interest Groups—the Unions

There was no strengthening of the councilmen's political base dur-ing the study. Consequently the council remained vulnerable to the demands of interest groups which could turn over a bloc of votes. While the level of political vulnerability remained unchanged, it was possible that the structure of interest groups was altered by fiscal stress, rendering them less able to make demands on city hall. The most important of these interest groups were the unions. Was the city able to weaken the unions by restructuring negotiations, rewriting contracts, or lowering salary and benefit increases? A trend toward weaker unions would bode well for future fiscal solvency by removing both one source of pressure for increased costs and a barrier to more cost-effective personnel deployment and promotion.

Contrary to expectations, fiscal stress actually strengthened the unions. The city manager's attempt to weaken the unions resulted in the 18% settlement in an arbitration case. Moreover, the lean years with no salary increase made the unions more demanding in later negotiations. In terms of management prerogatives, the negotiations did not succeed in reducing the unions' powers. As a result of low salary settlements the unions (encouraged by outside organizers) struck against the city in 1977. During the strike the unions forged a new solidarity with both noncity employees and other unions within the city. This solidarity led to a successful strike, and the union leaders were determined not to lose this new solidarity. It is doubtful that the prior tactics of management, to keep the unions squabbling and separate, will continue to work.

After several years of fiscal stress the unions were not only more unified but also more sophisticated in campaigning for candidates who would help them. While the unions had backed a losing candidate for mayor in 1974, in 1976 they won two council seats. These two councilmen were working from inside to reduce restrictions on employee political activities. The possibility of still greater increases in union power loomed ahead.

The Power of the City Manager

Part of the fiscal stress stemmed from the structural weakness of the city manager and his inability to keep apart the departments and the councilmen. The councilmen and department heads supported each other's requests and made it impossible for the city manager to cut the departments' budgets to levels permitted by anticipated revenues.

As a result of the fiscal stress, the political controversy over the parking decks, and the unions' successful strike, the city manager who had been appointed in 1972 was fired in 1977, just after the strike. Several months later, a new city manager was hired, an older, more experienced person with a reputation for firing all those who did not come up to his standards. After a few symbolic moves to indicate a new man at the helm, his first action was to reverse the policy allowing so much contact between department heads and councilmen. He forbade the department heads from any direct contact with councilmen and ordered all such communication to go through him. This was a crucially important step in curtailing budget deficits.

The new city manager then attempted to depoliticize the appointment of the police chief and fire chief. While most other department heads were appointed by the city manager, the police and fire chiefs were appointed by the Police and Fire Board. It in turn was controlled by the mayor and was his major structural source of power. The new city manager indicated that he himself should have appointive power over his department heads, and he won the issue. The chiefs of these crucially important deficit-generating departments thereafter reported to the city manager, which increased his power to cut their budget requests.

Since these trends toward isolating department heads and making them less political have been ongoing only since the new city manager took over in late 1977, it is too early to expect much change in the departments' budget requests. Moreover, there is not much information on departmental requests in the 1978 budget. One bit of information in the 1978 budget is the total amount cut by the city manager from the departments' budget requests. This amount, much smaller than in prior years, indicates that either the departments are submitting smaller budget requests or there is enough revenue to satisfy all their requests. Since the deficits were eliminated and the budget balanced for 1978, the possibility that the city manager allowed the departments large increases is unlikely. I infer then, that the new city manager had begun to curtail departmental requests.

The pattern of personnel cuts made by the city managers' in the departments' requests implied which departments had lost power. The Public Works Department (of which Streets is a part) submitted a request which was deeply cut, while Police and Fire succeeded in making a number of new hires. The city manager explained the increases in Police and Fire as necessary because of the new shopping center and the completion of the Fire Department's plan to add stations in new portions of the city. The city manager thus implied that these expansions, the results of prior decisions, had to be completed. However, he cut deeply into the budget request of the Public Works Department, the only one of the three departments running deficits whose head he had authority to fire at that time. He fired the Public Works director (an employee of the city for seventeen years) several months later. From these events it appeared that the ability of the city manager to cut departmental requests was related to his ability to hire and fire his department heads. The new city manager's success in wresting control from the Police and Fire Board over the hiring and firing of the police chief and fire chief thus appeared to be a very positive step toward financial recovery.

The trend toward a stronger city manager would seem to bode well for city finances. Unfortunately, there is an underlying model of politics in the city which suggests that if the city manager becomes too dominant, the whole form of government may topple.

The city's change from a commissioner form of government to a city manager form in 1955 was not complete. The city was split in its desire for reform, and for responsiveness (in the sense of doing favors for citizens). This split in the city reflected itself in the composition of the council, in which the mayor and two other councilmen came from the anti-reform faction. The city was reformed in structure but only partly reformed in content. This compromise seemed to satisfy the city, and it persisted through the 1950s and most of the 1960s. By the late 1960s a transition began from a de facto city administrator to a real city manager. It started with the choice of a brilliant but alcoholic city manager, who made only a moderate impact on city policy because of his personal problem. He was followed by a bright and well-trained city manager with virtually no experience. The most recent city manager was a very competent, experienced man. Each stage wrought substantial improvements in the city manager form. In the 1970s the shift to city manager government became a political reality when the mayor of twelve years, strong by dint of personality, was replaced by a conservative "weak" mayor, weak by dint of indifference to leadership qualities and lack of a personal following. After more than fifteen years, the city was finally achieving reformed government.

Not all the citizens wanted a city manager government. They had lived with the compromise which had evolved *because* it was a compromise. When the compromise fell apart, some citizens became restless. In 1972 there was a successful popular referendum to restructure the council elections from at-large to partly at-large and partly district candidates. This change reintroduced compromise between the strong mayor/alderman system, and the city manager/council form. The changes went into effect in 1975. The controversy over the parking decks renewed restlessness, and a public movement started to eliminate the city manager form entirely.

The stronger the city manager becomes, and the closer the system is to achieving its ideals, the stronger this movement to change the whole system is apt to get. In addition to pressure to change the whole system, there will also be pressure to get rid of the current city manager. The mutually beneficial alliance between department heads and the council will die hard. Threatened department heads may appeal to the council, which may or may not support the department heads. The actions of the city manager have been quick and sure, regardless of the antagonisms stirred up. So far, his actions have been condoned by the council but he may antagonize them as well. His career history to date has consisted of a number of very short terms in many cities.

This past experience suggests that the council may soon decide they are too hamstrung, that order has been restored, and they no longer need such a rigid regime. If this happens too soon, the permanence of the changes the city manager has introduced will be thrown into question.

The Council

While the degree of the city manager's control over the department heads is part of the problem of collusion between department heads and the council, the attitudes of the council itself is the other part. If the councilmen cease to press for special projects and will not tolerate an unbalanced budget, much of the pressure to generate deficits will disappear.

Whether there was any change in attitudes of the council was questionable. There were several indicators that the council had perhaps had a change of heart and was more concerned with the financial integrity of the city. For one thing, the council fired the former city manager and consciously avoided repeating the mistake of replacing him with a young and inexperienced assistant city manager. They chose not only an older man but one with a reputation of a "hatchet man," who ruthlessly cut out inefficient personnel everywhere he worked. Secondly, the councilmen, showing an increased awareness of budget limitations, asked whether there was money in the budget for specific items. They began to demand (and received) cost-benefit analyses on proposed annexations of land.

Despite their increased interest in revenue limitations, the council continued to illustrate the ideological split between the "do-nothings" and the "builders." The "do-nothings" opposed all expenditures, even for necessary projects, while the "builders" seemed relatively unconcerned with the cost of their projects. As soon as the emergency was over, it seemed likely that the battle between these roles would resume, and there would be alternating periods of under- and overexpenditure for capital projects.

The council's concern with slack resources,[3] their use, and re-creation supports this prediction of cycles of council behavior. In the early 1970s the council had its special projects and minimized the importance of deficits. As the importance of the deficits became clear, the council was curtailed in its projects. Councilmen complained they could not do anything for their constituents. In 1973 the council considered the shopping mall, an expansion that would provide immediate political credit and would ultimately increase revenues. In 1975 they considered rebuilding parts of the downtown, with similar intent. The development projects, especially the shopping mall, put a severe strain on the budget, with increased capital outlays and increased costs of public works, police, and fire. But they had the potential to re-create slack resources which could be used for special projects.

As further illustration of the pressure to re-create slack for political projects, the council in 1976 chose to put its own projects into the budget before the salary increases were determined. That means the council took its piece of the budget pie before the amount of slack could be determined and before the unions could gobble up any increased revenue. As a result, the amount of deficits unavoidably increased. Another example of the council's efforts to recreate slack was the creation of a position of grantsman to chase and apply for federal grants. Given the conservative antifederal government stance of most of the councilmen, this position was no small concession to the pressures of felt necessity.

The implications of this analysis are that at least some councilmen did not really care about the deficits but only about that portion of revenues marked for projects that they could take credit for. They did not want the city to go bankrupt, but they resented the enforced austerity of the recovery period. These councilmen were not interested in bureaucratic expansion per se. They were interested in expansion only as it facilitated the carrying out of projects and as it was necessary as a trade-off with department heads in order to get projects into the budget. Because they had so few other resources, councilmen interested in re-election had a deep and stubborn interest in special projects. Consequently, it seemed likely that old patterns would reassert themselves.

To summarize, the city is not yet home free. It has made some real accomplishments, which should not be minimized. It did eliminate enormous deficits within a period of three years. It did so in part by raising tax rates and in part by controlling expenditures. Expenditures were almost frozen for four years. The city improved its pension funds by increasing payments. It stopped annexing areas which would be a net financial drain to the city and began to annex revenue-producing areas. The city made some important organizational changes that strengthened the city manager and helped control one source of pressures for increased expenditures. From now on, however, developments will be touch-and-go. A complete chain of events will have to turn out positively to insure that the city will get back on its feet. If the new city manager stays in position long enough to cement changes by appointing his own department heads, if there is no recession in the near future, if the assessed valuations do not fluctuate or fall, if the city can meet debt repayments without additional tax rate increases, if the city can hang on until the shoppinig center generates new revenues, and if the new downtown attracts new businesses, then the city will have a chance to stabilize its finances despite some of the more intractable problems. Even if the city succeeds, it will not have done it entirely on its own. It received aid and encouragement from Moody's, from federal agencies, and from the state. Sometimes this aid was a mixed blessing, but it did help the city get through some of the worst portions of the crisis with minimum dislocation.

In this chapter it is clear that Southside offers no simple model of a self-correcting city in the sense that problems stimulate internal solutions. Rather, there seem to be some such corrective mechanisms embedded in cyclical political patterns that will get the city into and, unless the economic and social problems prove overwhelming, out of fiscal stress.

Eight

Theoretical
Implications

This final chapter is not a summary of results but a comparison of the three theoretical positions, outlined in Chapter 1 with the events observed in Southside, to show where the propositions predicted events and where they did not. The present chapter makes an overall evaluation of the three theoretical approaches, and suggests the limitations of the generalizability of both the existing theories and the case study. It also discusses an issue relatively neglected in the literature—the incentives for getting out of fiscal stress.

Comparison of the Literature and the Study

Let us reiterate the three hypotheses outlined in Chapter 1: (1) migrations were the major cause of fiscal stress; (2) bureaucratic growth caused fiscal strain; and (3) city hall's vulnerability to citizen and interest group demands caused fiscal stress.

The Migration Models

There were three different migration models: the first was that migrations of blacks out of the South into the cities of the Northeast and Midwest precipitated fiscal stress; the second was that out-migration of the middle classes to the suburbs caused fiscal stress; and the third was that interregional job and population shifts resulting from the decline of manufacturing caused fiscal stress.

The first model assumes that because of the lower average educational achievements of the black migrant group, their extreme poverty, and their difficulty in getting good jobs, they became a burden on local government both in social services and in police and fire services. Because the cost of servicing the poor pushed up taxes, the middle classes, reducing the tax base, rebelled and left the city. The combination of higher service costs and reduced tax base is said to cause fiscal stress.

I found that migrations of poor blacks to Southside contributed to fiscal stress, but not in the manner suggested in the literature. Since social services were not in the city budget, needs or demands of blacks for social services could not have been reflected in the budget. Moreover, most of the city's black families were employed, if only at menial tasks, and few were on welfare. Expanding ghetto conditions did aggravate the number of calls to the police, but the Police Department did not change the distribution of services to the black community on the grounds that crime rates were highest in the (white) downtown, not in black neighborhoods. Additional money was spent on police protection to protect whites against blacks but not to protect blacks from crime. Although police expenditures increased after the racial rioting in 1968, the city council did not raise taxes to pay for increased services. Consequently it cannot convincingly be argued even that blacks indirectly caused a rise in taxes by increasing fear among whites. Whatever prompted the middle classes to leave the city, it was not high tax burdens caused by serving the poor.

The second migration model argues that suburbanization causes fiscal stress. In this model city residents leave the city because they love newness and long for green spaces and their own homes. They may also leave the city to follow jobs or to avoid crime, bussing, and racially mixed schools. Central cities consequently lose their population. The decline leaves cities with high fixed costs to be supported on a shrinking tax base. Moreover, suburbanites continue to use city facilities without paying for them. These factors combined cause fiscal stress.

I found that suburbanization did play a role in Southside, but again not quite in the manner foreseen by the literature. The middle classes left the city at first for reasons not related to race, but later for fear of blacks and black slums. The city kept the revenue generated by these families, because it annexed the new suburbs. The annexations were expensive in capital and new service levels. There was no commensurate increase in the tax base because there was no increase in population, merely a redistribution and reduction of density. As much as any other single factor this increase in area explains the location of deficits in the budget and the reasons for year-to-year increases in expenditures.

The third migration model is concerned with the effects of interregional job shifts. It emphasizes loss of jobs due to the general decline of heavy industrial manufacturing, specifically in the Northeast and Midwest. Such a decline results in lower populations for a whole metropolitan area and reduces the tax base, directly through the loss of taxable businesses, and indirectly through reductions in sales taxes and property tax revenues. After businesses leave, there may be a period of high unemployment, which strains the relief capacity of the city.

The decline of the importance of manufacturing was an underlying theme in the city's fiscal woes. Of the half dozen or so comparable cities in the area, Southside had the lowest tax base to start with. Then several large employers left the area. General stagnation of business underlay the fiscal crisis on the revenue side. However, unemployment per se (independent of national recessions) was not yet a serious problem. Stagnation rather than decline in the number of jobs was important in generating fiscal stress. Equally important, the high-wage heavy industry had stopped expanding by the time the new migrants arrived from the south, which forced them into lower-paid jobs. This situation aggravated the housing problems and contributed to racial antagonism and growing slums. After the end of the study, one of the steel mills closed, which suggests that worse economic woes may occur in the future.

Growth of Bureaucracy

The second set of arguments explaining fiscal stress is presented by the Public Choice School of nonmarket economics. This school focuses on the growth of bureaucracy as the cause of fiscal stress and offers a series of mechanisms to explain that bureaucratic growth. These can be summarized as follows: (1) enlargement of the public sector through the absorption of functions better performed by the market place; (2) enlargement of the public sector through excessive citizen demands on existing functions because cost and benefit are divorced; (3) enlargement of the bureaucracy because administrators who wish to expand their departments control the political machinery which determines personnel and salary levels; and (4) excessive personnel buildup because federal grants mask its true cost.

The first of the Public Choice School's arguments is that governments have added functions best left to the private sector, where price can limit demands. Only those services which truly benefit the whole community should be in the public sector. Otherwise—and this gets into the second portion of their theory—because price and service levels are not closely related for individuals, they will demand too many public goods.

Southside did not expand its services during the period of buildup of fiscal stress or in the preceding decades. The city was and remained narrow in scope. There was perhaps some enlargement in the scope of departmental functions, but in only one case was it possible to identify a shift from private or individual costs to public costs. That case was the Fire Department.

The change in the Fire Department was nothing so dramatic as a shift from a volunteer company to a city-paid company, but it was nevertheless detectable. First, the Fire Department added an ambulance service in response to public dissatisfaction with the service delivered by private companies. This was surely a shift from the private to the public sector, and it certainly cost the city money. Whether its being public caused people to overuse the service was not yet clear. But, more important in terms of the proportion of deficits generated, the whole expansion of the Fire Department can be viewed in terms of shifting a cost from the private to the public sector. The fire chief wanted to achieve a better fire insurance rating, for which he needed to build new stations, to buy equipment for them, to staff them, and to set up reserve equipment. By improving the fire-fighting capacity of the city, the chief was reducing insurance costs which had been borne by individual citizens.

By putting the function in the public sector, Public Choice School theorists would argue, the relationship between cost and service is obscured. This undoubtedly happened, but without the untoward effect of increasing demand. People do not want an unlimited amount of improvement in city fire departments, especially since the cost of improving the services can outstrip the insurance savings. Most people probably take a city's fire rating for granted; it is usually the department rather than citizens who initiate improvements.

The shift of burden from citizen to city did in fact contribute to fiscal stress, but not because a private cost became a public one. The shift caused trouble because money that had been spent on insurance was not raised as local revenue to support a new level of service. This problem was not the result of the mechanism the Public Choice theorists emphasized.

The second mechanism proposed by the Public Choice theorists to explain the expansion of government is that individuals or small groups who are able to get services for themselves from established departments in fact share the costs with other taxpayers, who do not benefit. As a result, such services appear incredibly cheap to those who obtain them, so demand for them goes up. City government then expands to handle the demand.

There can be no doubt that there was some distribution of service to individuals or neighborhoods rather than to the city as a whole, especially in the public works area. Councilmanic special projects were frequently of this sort. The early phase of annexations was also said to benefit particular owners through the extension of city water and sewer to undeveloped parcels. Nevertheless, there is little evidence that departments expanded in order to carry out this kind of work. Rather, even the most politicized of department heads refused additional employees whose purpose would be to carry out special projects. The professionalism of the staff limited this kind of expansion. There was also a counter philosophy in the city that argued that those who benefit should pay. The downtown redevelopment project was largely funded out of special assessments. A special service district was created so that the higher costs of servicing the downtown would be borne by the merchants themselves. In short, while there was some distribution of services to individuals or groups, there was little evidence that such allocations enlarged demands and that government added personnel to fill the need. Rather, the limitations on personnel served to limit the amount of resources which could be distributed in this manner. The Public Choice theorists do not discuss this possibility because they do not consider professionalism apart from bureaucratism.

Another problem with the Public Choice School argument to the effect that the provision of separable goods generates excess public demand is that most of the demand for government expansion came from *within* city hall, from the departments, unions, and council.

The internal pressure for growth at city hall is consistent with the third Public Choice School mechanism for generating fiscal stress: that government always grows because (a) individuals in government personally benefit from a larger bureaucracy; and (b) government employees have the political power to create the growth that services their individual interests. Closer examination of the growth of government in Southside supports some portions of the Public Choice argument but modifies others.

Public Choice School literature has sometimes treated bureaucracy at such a level of abstraction that there seems to be only one group of actors—bureaucrats—who have desires to improve their own careers. The power that these bureaucrats have to expand their agencies is usually assumed to be voting power, ability to mobilize their subordinates, and clientele. This model may fit well with historical descriptions of patronage government at the national and local level, but it does not describe Southside very well.

In a reformed city government, where department heads are selected by the city manager rather than by the politicians, department heads control few votes, if any. In Southside, even in the more political departments, such as police and fire, the strength of the chiefs did not seem to derive from their control of voting blocs but rather from budget exchanges with councilmen. As for less overtly political departments, their strength with the council depended on willingness to do small favors for constituents, and even here, department heads frequently defied council members. In this unionized bureaucracy, department heads and organized employees perceived their interests separately and differed in resources and kinds of political exchanges.

Based on the case study, it can even be questioned whether the department heads always want to expand their departments. Prestige seemed to depend in part on the level of education of the staff and their capacity to do the job rather than sheer numbers. Department heads resisted council attempts to add unskilled employees to their departments. In the case-study city, bureaucracy got more expensive, but not always larger.

The mechanism of having enough political power to vote oneself a salary increase was apparent in the city unions if not among department heads. But the unions' capacity to operate formally in campaigns was limited by law, and it only became a formidable tool towards the end of the fiscal crisis. Since the late 1960s, however, the threat of political influence has given the unions an advantage and undoubtedly cost the city money. In this respect, the Public Choice School theory did describe the case-study city.

The fourth mechanism cited by Public Choice theorists to explain the expansion of government is that influx of federal funds at the local level makes the addition of new personnel seem less expensive than it is. The timing of the city's personnel growth coincided with federal grants in a way that suggests the Public Choice theorists may have been correct on this issue. There is no direct evidence in the study to prove or disprove the thesis, but the fact that revenue sharing funds were spent both on personnel and in the departments with budget deficits is suggestive if not conclusive. It could well be that the expansion would have taken place anyway and that federal funds helped to alleviate stress rather than encourage expansion. But if that is true, it leaves no explanation for the continued addition of personnel in the period of deepest deficits.

In short, the dominating image emerging from the Public Choice literature is that of a bureaucracy which always grows because growth serves the interests of those inside the bureaucracy as well as beneficiaries of policies. This growth is almost mechanical, and it starts as soon as a new program or department is added. Providing federal funds merely accelerates the process of growth by making it look cheaper.

By contrast, the case study suggests that viewing the bureaucracy as a single actor is incorrect, especially in a reformed city. Professional department heads, politicians, and unionized employees should be viewed as three different bureaucratic actors, each with different motivations. In Southside, the unionized employees wanted higher salaries; staffing levels were beyond their scope of bargaining. They enforced their salary demands with threats of political power exercised against elected officials. Department heads wanted more personnel, but were primarily interested in qualifications, seeking prestige through the educational attainment and ability of subordinates and seeking organizational slack in terms of excess intellectual capacity of their employees. Politicians sought growth of a different sort. On the one hand they wanted additional personnel, in the form of patronage appointments; on the other hand they wanted organizational slack in the form of money for capital expenditures. The opposing goals of professional department heads and politicians normally controlled overall levels of growth, because each blocked the other's demands. But during the case study, this opposition collapsed, and they cooperated to forward each other's goals. This was partly possible because of federal government grants.

The Public Choice theorists appropriately identified growth in the bureaucracy as a key cause of fiscal stress, but did not identify for Southside the mechanisms generating growth, with two exceptions: (1) the increase in federal nonearmarked revenues did seem to increase the number of new hires by making them seem cheaper; and (2) unionized labor did act as a voting bloc, at one point during the study, to raise its own salaries.

Political Vulnerability

The third set of arguments discussed here concerns the political vulnerability of city hall to demands. There are basically three positions: the first is that the strength of voter support for the mayor or council determines vulnerability to demands; the second is that the structure of government, especially its machine or reform characteristics, determines vulnerability to demands; and the third is that the strength and degree of organization of interest groups determines vulnerability.

The first premise predicts that a breakdown of voter coalitions may cause fiscal stress because politicians intent on rebuilding coalitions may spend too much money to woo voters. This argument receives considerable support from the study, since voter coalitions did break down with the predicted increase in spending to regain voter support.

There seemed to be two related trends that combined to break down voter coalitions. The first was the gradual demise of bloc voting as people became better educated and more individualistic. Labor, church, and ethnic group leaders became unable to deliver large blocs of votes. As this change occurred, the political machine died, and the city manager form took on reality. In the absence of party or slating organizations, with at-large elections it became increasingly difficult to gather a following. The elimination of patronage hiring, which followed the demise of the machine, reduced the resources available to build new voting coalitions. In this context the award of salary increases and benefits to municipal unions became increasingly important, because each union member received some direct benefit. Councilmen were not dependent on union *leaders* to turn over a bloc of votes.

One version of the voter coalition model specified the cause of the breakup of voter coalitions as the influx of blacks from the south. While this theory might have been applicable to some northern cities, it did not fit Southside. The impact of black migrants on established voter coalitions was limited for several reasons. First, for years the number of blacks in the city had been small, the number of registered voters low, and actual turnout at elections even lower. Elections, entirely at-large until 1975, made it unlikely for a candidate supported by blacks to be elected. Secondly, even when the number of blacks grew, the black community remained politically fractionated. Thirdly, blacks were not absorbed into the machine in the 1960s, and by the 1970s, the machine was gone. The candidates made no particular effort to woo or buy the black vote. Finally, whites who had left the city found themselves inside the city again as the suburban areas were annexed. Until 1975 candidates found the same basis of support as always, despite the outward migrations. In 1975 the at-large elections were modified, providing the possibility of black representation, but by that time, the fiscal crisis was already full blown, so whatever the impact of including blacks in the political process, it came after the origin of the fiscal crisis.

The second set of arguments explaining vulnerability to demands grows out of the reform literature. Its basic premise is that city manager government is more insulated from demands than machine government. While generally true, the thesis is hard to test because pure city manager government seldom exists. Southside was characterized by a series of compromises between reformed structure and nonreformed government. These compromises left the city more vulnerable to demands than either a full-blown reformed structure or a totally unreformed city. From the reformed tradition the city took nonpartisan at-large elections and an antipatronage bias; from the machine tradition it took a majority of the councilmen interested in getting reelected. The councilmen had neither natural constituencies nor party to appeal to for support because of the type of elections, and few resources with which to build coalitions because of the antipatronage bias. The result was their great vulnerability to demands by the city's organized employees.

The third argument concerning vulnerability assumes that the structure and strength of interest groups determines city hall's vulnerability. Any group of voters, such as businessmen, poor people, homeowners, historical preservationists, or environmentalists may be organized and poised to pressure city hall. The present study suggested that, while many of these interest groups were organized and active at city hall, their independent impact on the fiscal crisis was probably not as great as the internal alliance between department heads and councilmembers or as important as the political weakness of councilmembers.

For example, the labor unions were organized for many decades but did not win a contract until after the racial disturbances in 1968. Even at this point the unions were not militant, but they became more militant and unified in response to the actions taken during fiscal stress. Not until 1977 did the unions successfully elect a candidate to council. Their power was thus increasing throughout the period, but benefits to the unions, derived from their solidarity (rather than from the councilmen's weak electoral backing), could not have initiated the fiscal stress in the first place.

Similarly, the business community was not well-organized during the early periods of fiscal stress, although it became better organized (more inclusive) and more active during the fiscal crisis. Through the influence of a councilman and a lobbyist and through direct contact with city staff the downtown store owners and the banks managed to persuade the city to adopt a downtown renewal project. The degree of their organization and focus on a single issue undoubtedly affected their success. City hall became vulnerable to their pressure, as the theory suggests. However, this pressure was successful in 1977 for expenditures in 1978. Moreover, much of the cost was paid for by special assessments, special service districts, and bond sales. The impact on expenditures was so late and so limited that it could not have caused the fiscal crisis.

In contrast to the unions and the business groups, the poor were not well-organized. They were represented from time to time by the NAACP and later, after the 1975 redrawing of districts, by several councilmen. They placed broad demands on city hall, mostly beyond its scope. The total amount of local funds spent on the poor for increased services or social programs was very limited and in no way strained the budget or contributed to fiscal stress.

The study suggests, then, that well-organized interest groups may be able to extract resources from city hall, but that in the case study city the major interest groups either were disorganized and ineffective or were organized after the fiscal stress began. In particular, the unions' history suggests that their effectiveness was due less to their organization and political pressure than to the weakness and dependence of council members on them for votes.

Overall, the political vulnerability model was fairly descriptive of events in the city, although specific details of the theory missed the mark. Particularly important in creating vulnerability were two factors: the decline of voting blocs and the lack of structural supports and resources for politically ambitious councilmembers.

Evaluation of the Literature

When all three of the theoretical positions discussed in this chapter are taken together, they offer potential explanations for both revenue decline and expenditure growth and postulate a range of mechanisms for generating fiscal stress. The very breadth of the combined theory suggests that it might not be applicable in all situations. The thrust of this study has been to show why certain hypotheses did not apply in Southside. To a certain extent, these departures from the propositions simply suggest that the propositions do not apply in cases like Southside, but in some areas the inapplicability of the models suggests weakness in the arguments themselves.

Some of the theoretical arguments were devised on the basis of examination of one or a few cities without much attention to the major differences between cities. These arguments in particular failed to describe events in the case study city. For example, the association of migrations of poor blacks from the South to northern cities with higher service costs to meet the needs and demands of the poor is clearly applicable in some cities, but not in Southside. There were a number of reasons for this. First, many blacks, having stopped in other cities before they got to Southside, were fairly knowledgeable about urban life in the north. Secondly, the city was of narrow functional scope and so could not respond to needs such as health and education. Thirdly, only a small proportion of blacks were either unemployed or on welfare. The blacks found low-paying jobs, but they were employed.

A second example of a model which fits some cities but not Southside is the Public Choice School theory that city governments grow because officials have sufficient political power over clients and employees to force politicians to give their departments generous budgets. This model holds, perhaps, for an oid-style political machine, in which both the department heads and the employees are patronage appointments. But the model certainly does not apply to a reformed city where department heads are chosen for technical skills and where political campaigning of employees is proscribed by law. There should really be two models; one for machine and one for reformed government. These two forms are not structured alike with respect to the political power of department heads.

These two examples should suffice to show that models created to describe broad-scope or machine cities are unlikely to apply to Southside. Because these models are of limited applicability, they are not therefore useless or inaccurate. But there are some areas in which the results of the case study raise questions about the theoretical arguments themselves and how they were arrived at. Because the case study offers a different interpretation of the same basic variables, the possibility exists that the actual processes observed in Southside may be more descriptive of cities in general than the processes suggested by existing theory.

One example involves the role of unions in fomenting fiscal stress. In the study, the unions got a contract guaranteeing collective bargaining in 1969, and the fiscal stress began not long after. In 1975 the unions campaigned unsuccessfully for a mayoral candidate, and in 1977 they elected a councilmember. It is tempting to correlate increasing union strength as an interest group with increased personnel and salary levels, but on detailed examination of the evidence, the argument does not hold up. Staffing levels were never a negotiable issue and the unions never asked for manning clauses. The existence of an outcome satisfying to unions (more personnel) does not mean that the unions caused that outcome. In this case, increased personnel came from a totally different source. Moreover, when the unions did gain voting control, it was long after the onset of fiscal stress, in fact, in the middle of the recovery period. The unions' power source was not their own organization or solidarity or control over votes but the unwillingness of councilmen to make labor policy. Councilmanic unwillingness to offend the city's employees would have existed with or without unions. Given the outcomes, it is easy to overestimate the influence of the unions.

Another problem that might be involved in existing theories is the assumption that cost increases in basic services after ghettoization of blacks is necessarily due to servicing those blacks. Fire rates are higher in many black ghettos, as is the number of police calls. The study showed, however, that in Southside the major cause of increase in cost of fire service was an attempt to improve the city's fire rating, not an attempt to increase service to poor neighborhoods. The need to improve the rating was precipitated by the white exodus to outlying areas, which were then annexed. Extending services to these areas caused the costly expansion of the Fire Department. Police Department expansion seemed to occur primarily to protect whites from blacks rather than blacks from each other. In short, an alternative explanation for the increase in service costs was that ghettoization increased services to middle-class whites, not to ghetto blacks. This kind of allocation of services in reaction to blacks may be widespread; a closer look at northern cities is required.

To summarize this section, existing theories of fiscal stress are rich and useful guides, but further research is required to determine the limits of their applicability and to see whether some errors in interpretation might have crept into them.

The Self-Correcting City

The theory considered as a whole is very comprehensive. Yet the study suggested one area in which the theory might be extended, and that is the whole issue of getting out of fiscal stress. While individual theorists recommend particular policies to eliminate fiscal stress depending on the particular cause, they have little or nothing to say about how, why, or whether these policies will be implemented. One of the most significant aspects of the case study of Southside is that it showed not only how the city got into fiscal stress but also how the city managed to extricate itself. The process of getting out of fiscal stress highlights the cyclical patterns of politics in Southside and the self-correcting mechanisms involved.

The study points out that because of the importance of revenue increases in providing resources for political coalition formation, the cessation of growth in revenues brings the political exchange system to a grinding halt. One way to avoid the negative consequences of revenue stagnation is to run deficits. This strategy is clearly to the advantage of councilmen only so long as they can keep such deficits quiet. When combined with a strategy for regenerating the tax base to restore revenue growth, running deficits seems to be a reasonable short-term answer. However, since the deficits are hidden, there is no effective way to monitor and limit the amount of deficits, and they continue to grow. There seems to be no incentive to reverse the situation. Elected officials must deny the deficits, and yet as long as they deny the existence or importance of deficits, they can take no action to reduce expenditures and bring the budget into short-term balance. Councilmen lack the motivation to cut back expenditures on one hand and the credibility to do it on the other.

What actually occurred in Southside was that the efforts taken to regenerate the tax base involved borrowing in the capital market and brought the whole fiscal situation to public attention. Thereafter, the political incentive system reversed the pattern of behavior. Elected (and appointed) officials strove to deny blame and disassociated themselves from the deficits at the same time that they earnestly sought to eliminate deficits. Avoiding negative publicity became more important for a time than distributing political resources. The goal became restoring fiscal health as quickly as possible despite the sacrifices involved. And this the city did, with huge tax increases and frozen expenditure levels.

The study suggests that a city can get itself out of fiscal stress (or at least get the budgets back in balance), when those deficits are caused by political response to a stagnation or decline in revenues so long as that decline is seen as potentially reversible through redevelopment. Moreover, the elimination of deficits and the general financial recovery can be carried out without any major change in the degree of local autonomy, without an emergency financial control board or spinoff of functions to other governmental entities. This outcome offers some hope for other troubled cities.

Generalizability of the Case Study Results

Implicit throughout this chapter has been the idea that the way Southside got into and out of fiscal stress may also be descriptive of other cities. In what cities might the results be applicable? Southside represents smaller, reformed, narrow-scope, fiscally and socially conservative cities. The results of the study are unlikely to apply to the nations' large, highly politicized strong-mayor cities, like New York, Washington, and Boston. But the big cities with well-publicized financial problems are not the only cities experiencing fiscal stress. Southside may be representative of a group of other cities sharing some of the characteristics which framed both its fiscal crisis and its response to fiscal stress. In this section those underlying characteristics are laid out, their implications for the outcomes reiterated, and the likelihood explored that they are widely shared by other cities.

Social and Fiscal Conservatism

Southside was characterized by a particular brand of conservatism which helped to shape its fiscal problems. This pattern included too little investment in the city's infrastructure, reluctance to accept federal aid, and unwillingness to try to solve social and racial problems other than by escape (out-migration) and increased police (social control). Oakland, California, and Cincinnati, Ohio, are examples of other cities experiencing fiscal stress which have shared parts of this conserative orientation at times during the recent past.[1]

To illustrate what such a pattern looks like in financial terms, and to aid in picking out other cities with similar profiles, Southside was compared to 230 other U.S. cities of similar size (having a population of 50,000–100,000). The results are shown in table 8.1.

The data are crude and incomplete, but highly suggestive. It is a narrow-scope city, and so it raised less revenue from its own sources. Costs for social services, such as hospitals, parks, schools, or welfare, are not included in the budget. The conservatism of the city politicians is reflected in the low per capita intergovernmental revenues. This figure reflects narrow scope because there are no welfare payments, but it results also from a reluctance to seek federal money or participate in federal programs (this tendency had begun to change by the mid-1970s, but the city staff reported continued inhibition about seeking federal money in 1977). Fiscal conservatism (or ultraconservatism), also reflected in the low interest payments on debt, indicates a lack of willingness to borrow for capital needs. Costs for police are much higher than the average, and costs for the Fire Department are somewhat higher than average. It is not yet known how many cities which have this overly conservative bias are experiencing fiscal stress, but case studies of places such as Oakland and Cincinnati suggest that the pattern may not be all that rare.

Table 8.1
Expenditures and Revenues, 1975–1976,
Southside and Other Cities, Population 50,000–99,999[a]

Category of expenses and/or revenues	Per capita Average	Per capita for Southside	Southside/ Average Per capita
General Revenue	$307.59	$230.90	.75
Intergovernmental	100.74	50.20	.498
Federal government	36.91	19.78	.535
G. R. S.	14.07	13.72	.97
General Revenue—own sources	206.85	180.66	.87
General Expenditure	313.56	240.49	.73
Education	41.47		
Public Welfare	1.92		
Cash Assistance	.49		
Hospitals	11.10		
Police	36.62	53.62	1.46
Fire	26.78	33.95	1.26
Sewerage	25.85		
Parks and Recreation	20.96		
Housing and Urban Renewal	10.65		
Library	5.54	5.87	1.05
Financial Administration	6.21	3.76	.60
General Control	9.35	4.43	.47
Interest, General Debt	11.96	4.05	.33
Expenses, Personal Services	153.96	117.01	.76

Source: U.S. Census, *City Government Finances* Table 5, 1975–1976.
[a]There were 230 cities, pop. 50,000–99,999 in 1972

Narrow Scope

Southside offered only a narrow range of services. Schools, parks, housing, welfare, and transportation were all handled by other governmental agencies or special districts. As a result, there was little association between particular city services and particular clientele groups. The city was thus buffered from demands from the poor. Not only did this buffering affect which services grew in expenditures during windfall revenue growth, but it also affected the process of retrenchment. The services which expanded were police, fire and streets—not education, hospitals and welfare. This pattern is the polar opposite of New York City's growth pattern.[2] During decline, cutbacks in service levels were not hampered by protests from the poor. The closest the city came to providing social services was to provide funds from federal grants to private social service providers. During fiscal stress these funds were withdrawn from this purpose and spent exclusively to reduce deficits in the Fire Department. The finance director and the city manager simply told these private service providers that their requests were denied. In terms of patterns of growth and ease of managing retrenchment, Southside should be typical of other narrow-scope cities.

Sources of Expenditure Increases

The study of Southside concluded that a major portion of its financial problems were due to expansion of personnel and capital expenditures in the Police and Fire Departments, and to a lesser extent in the Street Department. Three factors seemed to underlie much of this expansion: (1) the increase in the percentage of black and Hispanic residents, along with increased ghettoization and racial tension, contributed to pressures for more police; (2) out-migration followed by annexation, increasing the city's area, diluted its fire services, while a new chief sought to improve the city's fire rating as a measure of his professional expertise; and (3) the availability of windfall federal revenues in the form of General Revenue Sharing and Community Development Block Grants made it easy to satisfy pent-up demands at deceptively low cost.

Police. The literature has shown that the police expansion experienced by Southside was also experienced by many other cities and for similar reasons. At the local level the response to riots was to increase police expenditures.[3] The response to an increase in the percentage of blacks was also an increase in the number of police.[4] The national trend was also followed in the state in which Southside was located: among the fourteen cities of over fifty thousand population in 1960, seven tripled or more than tripled the per capita costs of police between 1965 and 1975. Federal money was available and the climate was right for expansion of the police by the late 1960s.

Fire. In those same fourteen cities, there was also an increase in fire protection costs during the 1965–1975 period. One half of the fourteen were older central cities or suburbs which could not expand their area. The other half grew rapidly, four of them more than doubling their area in the 1960–1970 decade. Areal expansion was thus fairly common during that period. However, areal expansion did not correlate with increased Fire Department expenditures. But fire expenditures did expand; of the fourteen cities, ten had *greater* per capita expenditure increases in the Fire Department between 1965 and 1975 than Southside did. This analysis suggests caution in generalizing the pattern of Southside to other cities; factors other than areal expansion seem to enlarge Fire Department expenditures, and areal expansion may not be accompanied by increased services to new areas. Newspaper accounts suggest that professional chiefs' determination to improve the fire insurance rating may be one of the most important factors in the increase in Fire Department expenditures.

Windfall Revenues. The third factor in expenditure increase in Southside was the availability of windfall revenues, which encouraged expansion beyond local revenues. The general issue of windfall revenues and their effects has been widely discussed in the literature and documented at the federal level.[5] The federal grant programs of the 1970s affected almost every local jurisdiction. Because the data on how the windfall revenues were expended are not very reliable, the impact of windfalls on localities has not been documented very well.[6] Case studies of cities like Cincinnati indicated that use of windfall revenues for service expansion played a role in that city's financial problems,[7] and further study would undoubtedly reveal more examples.

Compromise between Machine and Reform Government. Much of what occurred in Southside took the form it did because the city's machine government gradually yielded to a reform government from the mid-1950s to the mid-1970s. The particular compromises that evolved between machine and reform politics were not always stable. For example, the city manager was structurally weak with respect to the department heads. There was no civil service structure, only a politicized personnel review board for police and fire appointed by the mayor, and there was no political party to aggregate interests and increase political participation. Politicians sought reelection, but had little control over patronage.

The underlying conditions that promoted these compromises have been widespread in the United States since the early 1950s. Big city machines have declined, not only because of increasing educational levels and declining ethnic identification, but because people have come to accept services as their due, not something deserving gratitude and loyalty.[8] Without such loyalty a machine cannot function. The decline of the importance of political parties has also been a general trend as nonpartisan elections at the local level minimize the importance of party labels. The increase in importance of narrow interest-group politics at the local level is one result of the demise of the party at the local level.[9] In short, the strain toward reform and the institutional void left by the machines may be expected to frame fiscal stress in many other cities.

Preconditions for Self-Correcting Cities

Self-correcting mechanisms are fairly common in fiscally stressed cities. There have been few municipal bankruptcies in the United States since the Great Depression, although cities have occasionally had financial problems.[10] Normally they reorganize their debt, increase revenues, and/or cut back their expenditure levels. Many cities have had serious financial problems during the 1970s which they have handled without major disruption.[11]

There were several preconditions necessary for self-correction to work in Southside, and these conditions may be present in many other cities.[12]

(1) The size of the actual or projected operating budget deficit must be clear or easily ascertainable to both internal actors and external actors.

(2) External lenders must be sensitive to changing fiscal circumstances and reflect worsening conditions in increased interest rates. Similarly, raters of bonds and notes must be responsive to changes in conditions because they often control interest rates.

(3) Officials, both elected and appointed, must perceive deficits and increasing interest rates as a waste of resources and an embarrassment both politically and professionally.

Besides these necessary conditions, it is also helpful if internal borrowing is visible and if those from whom revenue is borrowed fight to have it restored. Thus unions who keep an eye on pension fund contributions and department heads who insist on obtaining funds budgeted to them increase the political costs of internal borrowing.

Some of these preconditions are more likely to occur in city manager cities because of the emphasis on the manager's role in preparing a clear budget. This emphasis occurs because in the manager form, the budget is one of the major forms of accountability and substitutes to some extent for the responsiveness of the strong-mayor form. In highly politicized cities, whether they be manager or strong-mayor cities, the budget is apt to be obscured both internally and externally, so that appropriate feedback mechanisms do not occur.

Summary and Conclusions

In comparing Southside with the three approaches drawn from the literature, it became clear that portions of the theory did not apply to cities like Southside. It became increasingly necessary to develop a model of fiscal stress that would apply to small, conservative, narrow-scope city manager governments. While it is not clear from existing research how many cities there are like Southside, many of the underlying conditions which framed both the fiscal crisis itself and the city's response to it are fairly widespread. Should it turn out that there are many cities like Southside, the policy implications are enormous. Moderating or even reversing the policy of redistribution to the poor will have little impact on these cities, since they did not redistribute to the poor in the first place; but policies which strengthen the preconditions for self-correction should aid these conservative cities without restricting their local autonomy.

Appendix:
Field Methods

Intensive field work was carried out in 1976. One complete budget cycle was followed. Events of the budget cycle were observed, informants were identified and interviewed, and documents were collected and analyzed. The observation was applicable only to current events and procedures, but interviews had a retrospective element, and former actors were interviewed along with current ones. The documentary data was traced back to 1963 (where possible). An attempt was made to sketch historical background as well as to delineate contemporary events.

The first method of gathering data was collection of documentary evidence. The data available was rich and varied. The major financial documents used were budgets and auditor's reports, supplemented by memos from the finance director and city manager to the city council. Much economic data along with documentation of social change and city service levels were provided by city departments, by consultant's reports, and by grant applications. Chamber of Commerce reports supplemented the documentary material provided by the city departments. Historical materials on city racial problems and solutions were available (although not complete) in the public files of the city's previous mayor. Newspapers were used to supplement that information. The mayor's files from 1963 to 1972 were used. The city's documents were available from 1964 to 1977, although budgets before 1970 were so skimpy as to be incomparable to later data. The city also provided records of council meetings from the date of the city's incorporation onward, and personnel records by department from 1972 to 1976. The city council minutes were used selectively from 1969 on.

The second approach to gathering data was through interviews with current and past participants in city government. A number of the city's staff were interviewed, including the city manager, the personnel director, the fire chief, police chief, and city planner. Union officials were interviewed. Former politicians, such as an ex-council member and an ex-mayor, were interviewed to help delineate changes over time. Newspaper reporters covering city hall were also interviewed, as were lobbyists for active lobby groups. Many of the chief informants, such as the city manager, police union negotiator, and council members, were interviewed more than once. Some of the interviews were formal, at city hall; others were less formal, and took place in parking lots or coffee shops or at homes. The number of formal interviews is reported in table A.1.

The third approach to data gathering was through participant observation at city meetings, public hearings, and council committee ses-

Table A.1
Data Base: Formal Interviews

City manager	6
Finance director	1
Police chief	2
Fire chief	1
Community Relations	1
Asst. city manager	1
Planning	1
Personnel	1
Water & sewer	1
Press:	
Reporters	1
Council members	2
Ex-mayor	1
Ex-councilmen	1
Labor:	
Fire Union Negotiator	1
Pres. of fireman's local	1
Police negotiator	2
	24

sions. Regular council meetings were attended as well as pre-council discussion sessions and finance committee meetings. Other assorted meetings were also attended, such as a meeting of city staff with potential bidders, public hearings for revenue sharing funds, and a union meeting. Informal behavior before and after council meetings was closely observed. Many, but not all, meetings were attended. Council meetings regularly occurred two times a month, with a pre-council meeting for almost every council meeting. Since there was considerable overlap between the two, both were not always attended. Finance committee meetings were held irregularly. I missed two of these only so far as I know. The number and types of meetings attended is reported in table A.2.

Table A.2
Data Base: Meetings

Union meeting (strike call)	1
Budget committee meetings	10
Revenue sharing hearing	1
City staff and potential bidders	1
Meeting of dept. heads and council	1
Pre-council meetings	6
Council meetings	17
	37

Each of the three techniques of data gathering was used to check on information gathered by the other techniques, and to fill in missing pieces of narrative. Each presented distinct problems of validity. Validity problems were compounded by the fact that fiscal stress is normatively and legally forbidden, is expensive, and suggests incompetence. There was, therefore, a bias in the data towards concealment. Data collection was approached with a great deal of caution and much care was taken to validate information.

Researcher's Role

Initial access to the city was provided by an associate at the university who was a friend of the city manager. The city manager arranged access to other city staff and to committee meetings. He introduced me as a faculty member interested in learning about budgetary processes. At the committee meetings I had continually to redefine my role—I was mistaken for a reporter. The budget director was instrumental in dispelling this illusion and would introduce subjects of political sensitivity in my presence by saying, "Since the press is not here, we can discuss . . ." After a period of time, my presence was taken for granted and my absences noted with humor. My role at such meetings involved the minimum of participation; I occasionally asked a few questions for clarification during or after a meeting and once or twice volunteered information.

While the politicians sometimes mistook me for a reporter, the city staff had no trouble with the idea of a college professor completing research for a book. However, I had more education than any of the city staff, and they were slightly awed by a woman with a Ph.D. While this awe probably somewhat reduced the cameraderie, it also cut down on attempts to give glib or superficial answers.

The research role evolved differently with different informants. Union representatives were eager to have me take a side and distrusted my neutrality; I argued that I did not wish to decide one way or another until I had everyone's viewpoint. With the city manager, I eventually became something of an outside confidante about his fears for losing his job. For the budget director, I was primarily a pest, an irritant, requesting time and documents, requiring courtesy, yet forever seeking discrepancies and explanations. Overall, the research role was quite satisfactory; I was identified with no particular faction, I had access to many records, and I could walk into any city department and request an interview. I was treated seriously, and many actors seemed grateful for the opportunity to get across their side of the story. By the end of the study, informants came to me asking to be interviewed. No one refused to be interviewed (but I did have to make one substitution when an informant had a heart attack).

Budget Data

Fiscal stress put considerable pressure on city officials to distort the budget. Budgets could not always be taken at face value. It is necessary therefore to explain how the budgets were analyzed.

Because it takes considerable skill and continuity in office to manipulate a budget, a search through several years of the budget will often reveal inconsistencies if they exist. The presence or absence of inconsistencies and the nature of the inconsistencies were used as data. Changes in the format of the budget over time were frustrating because they made the data incomparable, but each change indicated a different emphasis or strategy of the manager. Also, if the budget was too pat, it was assumed that the budget had been manipulated. At least one of the budgets used in the study—the one that reportedly contained hidden deficits—was impossibly pat. Interviews confirmed that it was a fudged budget. This budget was ignored as a source of hard data, but the fact that it was fudged was considered evidence in unraveling the causes of fiscal stress. Moreover, because hiding the deficits was part of the problem in the early years, estimates of budget deficits were taken from administrators, not directly from the budgets.

Despite some distortions in the budget, it was a most useful document in a number of ways. First, it provided the fund structure; that is, which departments were in the general fund and which outside. Second, it provided line item budgets, with detailed breakdowns on all capital items and personnel. Each authorized position was listed separately each year by fund account with its classification and salary. This kind of budget detail made it possible to check out some of the arguments about increases in hospitalization insurance (they were due more to increases in staff than to increases in the cost of coverage). Third, it was possible to check out the source of budgeted increases in expenditures by fund, as described in chapter 2. Fourth, budgets also provided a record of departmental budget requests, city manager recommendations, and council action. The city manager argued that these were accurate records of actions taken, and since he admitted other ways in which budgets were distorted or manipulated, there is no reason to question his statement. Consequently, it was possible to trace through how high or low the departments' requests were, how much the manager cut, and whether the council raised or lowered the city manager's recommendations. Since most of the budget negotiations took place in informal sessions at which the manager was informed what not to cut, occasions in which the manager did cut, though the council restored the funds, show both the extent of the battle put up by the city manager and the fact that he lost. Fifth, the budgets often provided a record of previous years' actual expenditures, against which the budgets could be compared. Finally, the budgets provided fairly detailed breakdowns of anticipated and actual revenues by source.

To summarize, financial information was used skeptically, in part because it tended to become less informative as there was more financial manipulation to hide. But this very process of obfuscation was suggestive of what was going on and of who must have known about it. And there was a great deal of financial material available that no one had motivation to distort or that could be profitably used in combination with other sources of information.

Interviews

If financial data had to be approached with care to establish validity, this was even more the case with interviews, especially with those people clearly involved with the creation of deficits. To guard against obvious falsehood, several steps were taken. Most of the background financial data was gathered first, to provide a buffer against glib answers. Secondly, all key informants were approached through intermediaries. Third, it gradually became clear to informants that no information leaked through the researcher, so information was more readily offered. Despite this caution, many of the responses to direct questions were geared to deflect blame onto other groups of actors. The consistency in type of answer by role was very clear. To compensate somewhat for this biasing element, all three groups of actors—politicians, city staff, and organized labor—were asked similar questions, and their answers were compared. Many of the key informants were interviewed more than once to follow up on inconsistencies and build on previous interpretations. Informal interviews were used to follow up formal ones. Finally, all information gained from the interviews was checked for consistency with other types of data. To increase the willingness to talk openly, informants were promised anonymity. The best interviews in terms of quality of information were indirect ones describing city procedures and informal ones following emotional experiences. A department head venting his spleen because he could not get hold of his budget was vivid testimony of internal borrowing. A city manager complaining that he was afraid he would lose his job over a fight with the council was evidence of why he could not cut the size of deficits.

Participant Observation

The third set of techniques for gathering data involved participant observation at city meetings. Difficulties included the questions of how much of what was observed was staged, and what proportion of the action was public. A variety of techniques were used to answer these two questions. First, comparisons were made between pre-council meetings and formal meetings to see how much was rehearsed. Secondly, councilmen were asked how many hours a week they spent on council business; limited hours suggested few out-of-view meetings. The amount of conferring before and after scheduled meetings was also taken to suggest limited time spent on politics while away from city hall. Informal reports of meetings outside city hall tended to imply individual councilmen had drinking relationships with union leaders and city staff more than with each other.

Several factors militated in favor of the validity of observations taken at city meetings. One was the legal requirement that all meetings of a majority of the councilmen must be reported to the press in advance; the second was the fact that all council members were serving almost *gratis*. Because they had to spend so much time on council business and also to earn their livings, time for outside meetings was limited. Thirdly, compromises were reached at pre-council sessions that were later acted upon. The compromises were worked out in public sessions; it would not be necessary to suppose that other secret sessions were held to work out compromises.

Overall Validity

In short, considerable effort was made to ascertain biases and discount for them, to check data between sources and over time, and to allay mistrust through the use of intermediaries, promises of anonymity, and lack of leaks over time. As a further test of the overall validity of the results, papers taken from the study were presented at conferences of academics and practitioners. Discussions with city officials about the research indicated that the verisimilitude of the overall picture was acceptable to those who live with fiscal problems on a daily basis.

The issue of validity of data under circumstances in which actors have motivation to minimize problems, distort data, and deflect blame was perhaps the most crucial methodological issue for the case study analysis. There were also other issues on which methodological decisions were made, which were sufficiently broad to affect the acceptability of the results. The first dealt with the priority given to local conditions rather than national trends; the second dealt with what constituted an acceptable explanation of financial stress.

Priority of Local Conditions

The assumption is made here that local conditions generating fiscal stress rather than national trends should be examined first and most thoroughly. Economists tend to treat national (or even regional) trends, such as recession and inflation, by first accounting for them and treating unexplained variation as locally caused. There are several reasons for not accepting this mode of analysis. First, it tends to be deterministic in its policy implications and concentrates on what cannot be changed rather than what can be changed. Second, it tends to put too much into the category of "inflation." Inflation includes all price increases whether these are forced on the city by higher labor costs in the private sector (uncontrollable) or whether they result from clumsy handling of labor negotiations (controllable). Third, there is an element of circularity in use of national trends as causes of local conditions, since frequently the commonness of local conditions causes widespread events which are then called national trends. By concentrating on the local level, one can better determine what is imposed on the city by external conditions and what it does itself. Fourth, there is a danger of committing an ecological fallacy, applying aggregate level results to the local level. While the economists are in no danger of doing this, since they tend not to apply their results at the local level, politicians who blame national trends for local events may be committing a logical error.

To give an example of the benefits of this assumption of local priority in case study analysis, there was a recent article in a local newspaper describing an increase in insurance rates to cities. On the face of it this appeared to be a cause of "inflation," an increase in cost of goods and services which cities must purchase. As such, these price increases would be out of the control of cities. In Southside, however, it turned out that the city had an extremely high accident and hospitalization rate and was past due in its payments when the increase hit. The late bills resulted from prior financial practice, the deficits and cash flow problems, much of which could have been avoided. The accident and hospitalization rate stemmed from poor training and a nonexistent safety program, which were amenable to improvement. The city improved its performance and lowered the rate of increase in insurance rates.

In short, it is better to avoid a priori assumptions about the effect of national trends. Instead, the local case should be examined while watching for situations in which outside agencies force changes or make decisions or cause cost increases. One has the advantage in a case study of being able to focus directly on the interplay of external forces and internal responses.

Violating Parsimony

The second methodological assumption, also consistent with case study approaches, is to violate the norm of parsimony. That is to say, rather than stop at the first probable explanation for fiscal stress, all of them *and* their interactions over time are explored. Such an approach must underlie specification of more quantitative models of urban fiscal stress. Otherwise, researchers do not know what variables to include in their models and are puzzled when several different models explain the same amount of variation and there is no statistical way to choose between them. Moreover, quantitative models at this point give very little feeling for interactions between variables. Hopefully, this case study will both inspire and inform such quantitative research in the future.

Notes

Chapter 1

1. American Enterprise Institute, *The Financial Crisis of Our Cities*, (Washington, D.C.: American Enterprise Institute for Public Policy Research, 1975).

2. Irene Rubin, "Extent and Causes of Fiscal Stress," unpublished paper, 1976. Fiscal stress was measured by excessive long term debt per capita, short term debt outstanding at the end of the year and the level of tax effect. Richard P. Nathan and Charles F. Adams, Jr., *Revenue Sharing: the Second Round* (Washington, D.C.: Brookings Institution, 1977), offer a similar operational description of fiscal stress, including (1) rising and uncontrollable costs, (2) recently imposed new taxes or changes in existing tax sources, (3) tax delinquency, (4) short-term borrowing, (5) reactions to proposed bond issues, and (6) public employee pay rate scales.

4. The city is given a fictional name to preserve the anonymity of informants; scholars who need to know the name of the city for research purposes are invited to contact the author.

5. See William Kornblum, *Blue Collar Community* (Chicago: University of Chicago Press, 1974), for a good description of this type of community.

6. The city of Oakland, California, provides an interesting comparison to the case study city. A somewhat larger city than Southside, it nevertheless is similar in some key ways: it has a reformed government, a limited tax base and a large minority population. It has experienced chronic financial problems. As in the case study city, the expansion of the police department and the costs of salary increments for police made it the city's largest and most expensive department in terms of manpower. Since the fire department was pegged to police, it also received increased salaries and benefits. The timing of the expansion seemed to be related to racial disturbances. For more on the Oakland situation, see Arnold Meltsner, *The Politics of City Revenue* (Berkeley: University of California Press, 1971).

7. See, for example, Advisory Commission on Intergovernmental Relations, *City Financial Emergencies* (Washington D.C.: USGPO, 1973); Richard Nathan

and Charles Adams, "Understanding Central City Hardship," *Political Science Quarterly* 91 (Spring 1976): 47–62; Touche-Ross and Co., *Urban Stress: A Comparative Analysis of 66 U.S. Cities* (New York: Touche-Ross, 1979); Terry Clark et al., "How Many New Yorks," Center for Study of Comparative Community Decision-Making, University of Chicago, 1976, (Mimeographed); Rubin, "Extent and Causes"; Michael Greenberg and Nicholas Valente, "Recent Economic Trends in Major Northeastern Metropolises," in *Post-Industrial America: Metropolitan Decline and Interregional Job Shifts*, pp. 77–100, ed. George Sternlieb and James Hughes (New Brunswick, N.J.: Center for Urban Policy Research, Rutgers, The State University of New Jersey, 1975); J. R. Aronson and A. E. King," Is There a Fiscal Crisis Outside New York City?" *National Tax Journal* 31 (June 1978): 153–163. These studies come to no conclusion other than that while New York is extreme, other cities are also in trouble. The debate is over how many other local governments are in trouble.

8. For examples of studies concerning multiple causes of fiscal stress, see Clark et al., "How Many New Yorks"; or Terry Clark and Lorna Ferguson, *Political Leadership and Urban Fiscal Policy* (N.Y.: 20th Century Fund, forthcoming). Most studies have dealt with only one or two causes. For example, on the effects of inflation, see John Ross and Susannah Calkins, "The Economic Stimulus Package at MidStream: The Role of State and Local Government," *Publius* 9 (Winter 1979): 45–66; Robert Crider, "The Impact of Inflation on the State and Local Economy," Academy for Contemporary Problems, Urban and Regional Development Series no. 5, 1978; David Greytak and Bernard Jump, "Inflation and Local Government Expenditures and Revenues: Method and Case Studies," *Public Finance Quarterly* 5 (July 1977): 275–301; and Normal Waltzer and Peter Stratton, "Inflation and Municipal Expenditure Increases in Illinois," Macomb, Ill.: Illinois Cities and Villages Municipal Problems Commission, Public Policy Research Institute, Western Illinois University, 1977. While the authors may totally agree with each other, they concede that inflation is not the sole problem of urban fiscal stress. Additional studies have dealt with tax elasticity and recession: for example, see Robert Crider, "The Impact of Recession on State and Local Finance," Academy for Contemporary Problems, Urban and Regional Development Series no. 6, 1978. For a review of the numerous studies on tax limitations see Charles H. Levine and George Wolohojian, "The Management of Fiscal Stress: A Study of Cutback Policies in Six Cities," College Park, The Institute for Urban Studies, University of Maryland, 1979 mimeographed. Also see "Proceedings of the Conference on Tax and Expenditure Limitations," in the special issue of the *National Tax Journal* 33 (1979). For studies on tax base erosion as the cause of fiscal stress, see especially Roy Bahl, Alan Campbell, and David Greytak, *Taxes, Expenditures and the Economic Base: Case Study of New York City* (New York: Praeger, 1979); and Sternlieb and Hughes, eds., *Post Industrial America*. On the effects of unionization, see Harry Wellington and Ralph K. Winter, *The Unions and the Cities* (Washington, D.C.: The Brookings Institution, 1971); Orley Ashenfelter," The Effect of Unionization on Wages in the Public Sector: The Case of the Firefighters," *Industrial and Labor Relations*

Review 24 (January 1971): 191–202; Ronald Ehrenberg and Gerald Goldstein, "A Model of Public Sector Wage Determination" Journal of Urban Economics 2 (1975): 233–245; and Ronald Ehrenberg, "Municipal Government Structure, Unionization and the Wages of Firefighters," Industrial and Labor Relations Review 27 (October 1973): 36–48. These studies on the effects of unions have been nondeterminate, partly for methodological reasons. Some studies have focused on intergovernmental revenues as a cause of local fiscal stress; for example, Advisory Commission on Intergovernmental Relations, Federal Grants: Their Effects on State and Local Expenditures (Washington, D.C.: USGPO, 1978); General Accounting Office, Federal Seed Money: More Careful Selection and Application Needed (Washington, D.C.: GAO, 1979); and Charles H. Levine and Paul Posner, "The Centralizing Effects of Austerity on the Intergovernmental System," paper presented at the American Political Science Association meetings, Washington, D.C., 1979. Finally, one other approach has been to explore the impact of annexations on urban fiscal stress; see, for example, Thomas Muller and Grace Dawson, The Impact of Annexation on City Finances (Washington, D.C.: The Urban Institute, 1973).

9. The best known mathematical models are D. F. Bradford and H. Kalejian, "An Econometric Model of Flight to the Suburbs," Journal of Political Economy 53 (1975): 195–207; S. W. Forrester, Urban Dynamics (Cambridge: M.I.T. Press, 1969); and Harry Richardson, Urban Economics (Hinsdale, Ill.: Dryden Press, 1978).

10. For another way to categorize the theoretical literature relevant to urban fiscal stress, see Richard Rich, "The Complex Web of Urban Governance: Gossamer or Iron," American Behavioral Scientist 24 (November/December 1980): 277–298. Rich divides the literature into an institutional approach (Public Choice School), a behavioral approach (interest group pluralism), and a structural approach (critical school or neo-Marxist). Rich's categories are more exclusively derived from political science literature than are the categories I use. I have expanded the scope of the discussion to include the impact of migrations and economic base erosion because the literature uniformly agrees that they have been important causes of local fiscal stress. I have not emphasized the structuralists' arguments for two reasons. First, they tend to be deterministic and offer no solution to urban fiscal stress other than a radical restructuring of the social system. Secondly, the structuralists emphasize the dual role of the state as the cause of fiscal stress by facilitating capital accumulation and buying off the unemployed and underemployed. These functions tend to be performed more frequently at the state and national levels than at the local level. The argument is less relevant to the local level, especially to small cities that perform no welfare functions. Nevertheless, some aspects of these functions were performed in the case study city, and the reader is invited to add the structural explanation of the case study to those described in the text.

11. This argument was summarized by Richard H. Cloward and Frances Fox Piven," The Fiscal Crisis: Who Got What, Why?" in idem, The Politics of Turmoil: Essays on Poverty, Race and the Urban Crisis (New York: Vintage,

1974). With this thesis, however the authors disagree, arguing that although demands of the poor increased, there was very little increase in service costs, with the exception of welfare. Werner Hirsch et al. in *Fiscal Pressures on the Central City: The Impact of Commuters, Nonwhites, and Overlapping Governments* (New York: Praeger, 1971), also explored the hypothesis that an increased number of poor blacks heightened costs but the study found little net effect on costs other than those of the police department. The police expenditure variable was sensitive to *changes* in the percentage of blacks, not to whether that percentage was high or low. This result suggests a fear reaction on the part of whites rather than a great need for service by blacks. The only study which confirmed a relationship between greater numbers of the poor and city expenditures for social services to benefit them was Gustely's work on New York City (Richard Gustely, "The Components of Change in New York City Government Labor Costs 1965–1972: Police, Fire and Environmental Protection" working paper #4 of the Maxwell School Project on Public Finances of New York City, Syracuse University 1972 and "The Components of Change in New York City's Labor Costs 1965–1972: Social Services, Public Schools and Higher Education" working paper #6 of the Maxwell School Project on Public Finances of New York City, Syracuse University, 1973.)

12. A standard version of the suburbanization/tax base erosion argument is outlined by Roy Bahl et al., "The Impact of Economic Base Erosion, Inflation and Employee Compensation Costs on Local Government," Occasional Paper no. 23, Metropolitan Studies Program, Maxwell School of Citizenship and Public Affairs, Syracuse University, 1975. Another approach to the fiscal impacts of suburbanization is Hirsch et al., *Fiscal Pressures* (New York: Praeger, 1971), which exlores the impact of commuters, nonwhites, and overlapping governments.

13. A series of fine essays on various aspects of this shift in population can be found in Sternlieb and Hughes, *Post Industrial America.* See also Edgar Rust, *No Growth: Impacts on Metropolitan Areas* (Lexington, Mass.: D.C. Heath, 1975).

14. See Wilbur Thompson, "Economic Processes and Employment Problems in Declining Metropolitan Areas" in Sternlieb & Hughes, (eds.) *Post Industrial America*, p. 189.

15. For one version of this argument, see Roy Bahl, ed., *The Fiscal Outlook for Cities: Implications of a National Urban Policy* (Syracuse, N.Y.: Syracuse University Press, 1978.)

16. The Public Choice theorists have written extensively on the urban fiscal crisis, perhaps because it seems to prove their theses. The early theoretical work on "fiscal equivalence," which is the matching of services provided and taxes paid in a small geographic area, can be found in Mancur Olson, "The Principle of 'Fiscal Equivalency': Division of Responsibility Among Different Levels of Government," *American Economic Review* 59 (May 1969): 479–487; and in Vincent Ostram, Charles Tiebout, and Robert Warren, "The Organiza-

tion of Government in Metropolitan Areas: A Theoretical Inquiry," *American Political Science Review* 55 (December 1961): 831–842. Some of the other key ideas are found in James Buchanan, *Public Finance in the Democratic Process* (Chapel Hill: University of North Carolina Press, 1967), and in Gordon Tullock's review of *Bureaucracy and Representative Government* by William Niskanen, in *Public Choice* 12 (Spring 1972): 119–124. In *Bureaucracy and Representative Government* (Chicago: Aldine-Atherton, 1971), Niskanen argued that those who wanted a higher spending level created a more active interest group to raise spending and frequently got much of what they wanted because they controlled agendas. More recent work has attempted to test some of the theory or to make it testable. See, for example, R. Croswell, "Self-Generating Growth in Public Programs," *Public Choice*, 21 (Spring 1975): 91–99; A. T. Peacock and J. A. Wiseman, "Approaches to the Analysis of Government Expenditure Growth," *Public Finance Quarterly* 7 (January 1979): 3–23; Thomas Bordcherding, ed., *Budgets and Bureaucrats: The Sources of Government Growth* (Durham, N.C.: Duke University Press, 1977); and John Meyer and John Quigley, eds., *Local Public Finance and the Fiscal Squeeze: A Case Study* (Cambridge, Mass.: Ballinger, 1977). Anthony Downs can also be considered part of this school; he assumes many of the same dynamics of bureaucratic growth though unlike some other Public Choice theorists he also assumes a limit to growth posed by those in competition with the organization for resources. See Anthony Downs, *Inside Bureaucracy* (Boston: Little, Brown, 1967).

17. The view that migrations of blacks and the exodus of whites broke down longstanding coalitions which had to be rebuilt is maintained by Cloward and Piven, "The Urban Fiscal Crisis." A somewhat broader statement of coalition building and vulnerability to interest groups is developed by Martin Shefter in "New York City's Fiscal Crisis: The Politics of Inflation and Retrenchment," *The Public Interest* 48 (Summer 1977): 99–127.

18. The relationship between reformism and vulnerability to demands is best stated in Robert Lineberry and Edmund Fowler, "Reformism and Public Policies in American Cities," *American Political Science Review* 61 (September 1967): 701–716. The current emphasis on business management as a way of eliminating fiscal stress is reflected in David Rogers, *Can Business Management Save the Cities: The Case of New York* (New York: Free Press, 1979).

19. On the relationship between social classes and political outcomes, see especially Edward Banfield and James Q. Wilson, *City Politics* (Cambridge: Harvard University Press and M.I.T. Press, 1963). For a more explicit linking of class, interest groups, and fiscal outcomes, see Clark and Ferguson, *Political Leadership.*

20. The presentation of the data is not intended to provide alternative explanations for them; see Graham Allison, *The Essence of Decision: Explaining the Cuban Missile Crisis* (Boston: Little, Brown, 1971). Rather, it is intended to provide a series of explanations, all of which are true, and to order them temporally. The chapters are also arranged to reflect the process of field work.

First, the "objective" material, which can be analyzed at a distance, is presented; secondly, the obvious and quantifiable factors (economic base erosion and migrations) are discussed; thirdly, the less obvious factors (political and administrative processes), which take more time to observe, are analyzed.

Chapter 2

1. Because of cash flow problems, the city finance director, who handled water bills for the Water and Sewer Department, deflected water revenues for other purposes to be repaid from sources that came in at less frequent intervals. This practice reduced the city's needs to borrow for cash flow purposes. It gradually became clear, however, that part of the borrowed funds were not repaid from other revenues. The director of the Water and Sewer Department hinted broadly that he could not get hold of his budget. The city manager later confirmed the occurrence of such "borrowing" without repayment. The debt was eventually repaid from a bond. This long-term debt was being used partly to cover operating costs of the city.

2. The overall revenue picture was more relevant here than the revenue by fund, although ultimately revenue and expenditure must match by account. The reason that overall revenue was more salient was that only a portion of the money for police protection and streets were from earmarked revenues. The rest was dependent on revenues which could be transferred between accounts. A revenue shortfall was like having a short blanket—either one's feet or one's chest gets cold—either there is a deficit in the Fire Protection fund or in the Police Protection Fund. Revenue sharing funds were this sort of movable revenue, which could be used to cut deficits in the Police, Fire, or Street Departments. The actual amount of revenue shortfall in any particular fund was thus somewhat manipulatable, although the sum of deficits was less manipulatable.

3. The decline in sales value of the downtown area was calculated by a county official and reported to me in January, 1977, by the assistant city manager. The total impact of stagnation of assessed values was muted by a state mandated program to raise the ratio of assessed to sales value of property. When this program reaches its target, the effect of the eroding tax base will be more drastic if the city has not managed meanwhile to stimulate growth.

4. That the county was retaining city revenues to avoid borrowing was reported to me by the county director of finance.

5. Salary increments were calculated as the difference between average *wages* in same department for two consecutive years. When detailed data was available, wages for identical positions for two consecutive years were compared. The advantage of using either calculation over using union wage settlements was that it accounted for the mix between unions in a single department and also included nonunionized positions. These figures did not

include longevity increases or overtime. Salary increases calculated as described could have been closely approximated in each department by using a
weighted average of union settlements, but to do so all the departments'
positions had to be listed and divided into unions. This was not possible for
each year.

Chapter 3

1. The importance of growth in business to generate city population growth
and prosperity is emphasized in the "stages of growth" models in urban economics, of which perhaps the best known is by Wilbur Thompson, *A Preface
to Urban Economics: Toward a Conceptual Framework for Study and Research* (Washington: Resources for the Future, 1963). The importance of job
loss as a measure of structural weakness in urban economies has been emphasized in the literature on New York City and on interregional job shift in
general. See Greenberg and Valente, "Recent Economic Trends," as an example. Population growth and decline is emphasized (but not exclusively) by
Sternlieb and Hughes, ibid.; by Thomas Muller, *Growing and Declining Urban
Areas* (Washington, D.C.: Urban Institute, 1975); and by Edgar Rust, *No
Growth: Impacts on Metropolitan Areas* (Lexington, Mass: D.C. Heath, 1975).
Areal growth and its impacts is discussed by many authors. The Advisory
Commission on Intergovernmental Relations in *City Financial Emergencies*
(Washington, D.C.: USGPO, 1973) emphasizes the importance of annexation
followed by lack of revenue growth. Muller and Dawson, in *The Impact
of Annexation*, argue that annexation precedes population growth. Physical
growth and decay is discussed as a separate phenomenon in the literature on
housing and other infrastructure. Of particular concern has been the deterioration of housing and the creation of slums. See Richard Muth, *Cities and
Housing* (Chicago: University of Chicago Press, 1969), for one example; or
Roger Ahlbrandt and Paul Brophy, *Neighborhood Revitalization: Theory and
Practice* (Lexington, Mass: Lexington Books, 1975), for a different analysis.

2. The literature on the relationship between city growth in business and
population on the one hand and area on the other is summarized and cri-
tiqued in Harry Richardson, *Urban Economics* (Harmondsworth, Middlesex,
England: Penguin, 1971), pp. 64–72.

3. The relationship between population decline and physical decay has
been debated in the literature, since an argument can be made for the opposite
case—that population growth and increased density cause physical decay.
The filtering theory of housing associated with W. C. Grigsby, *Housing Markets and Public Policy* (Philadelphia: University of Pennsylvania Press, 1963),
assumes that lack of demand causes decay in neighborhoods, and that a constant flow of new poor migrants will keep up the market for older housing and
make it financially feasible to remodel and recycle such housing. With respect
to the impact of out-migration of the middle classes to the suburbs, Heinz

Kohler, in *Economics and Urban Problems* (Lexington, Mass.: D.C. Heath, 1973), states the case for declining population leading to physical decay: "What is left behind in the central cities then is all too often a permanently depressed economy that has ceased to share or share fully in the natural rate of growth. Net investment is likely to be lower than average . . . more often than not, the area's total Capital Stock (industrial plant, housing, streets and public buildings) is allowed to deteriorate" (p. 79). On the relationship between declining demand for housing and neighborhood decay, see Ahlbrandt and Brophy, *Neighborhood Revitalization*, pp. 5–22.

4. Robert Bish, "Balancing Benefits and Costs in Local Fiscal Decision Making," Paper presented to the American Society for Public Administration, Phoenix, 1978; and Edgar Rust, *No Growth*, discuss the implications of migration when unemployment is high.

5. The application of the city government for a Community Development Block Grant contained data on fire and police calls by neighborhood for two time periods. These data indicate perceptible increases in fire and police calls in developing ghettos of the city.

6. The design and location of patrols was determined by examining consultants' reports on the Police Department in 1965 and 1969. The city's patrol zones were large and almost equal in territory despite emerging differences in the ethnic composition and income within them. Moreover, there were constant and well-publicized complaints from the poorer black neighborhoods that police responded very slowly, if at all, to their calls. In trying to respond to these complaints, the mayor sponsored a police substation in the problem neighborhoods. The Police Department successfully resisted this initiative, even though it would have meant expansion. Police came to associate these neighborhoods with antipolice attitudes and physical danger, and avoided them when possible.

7. In *Growing and Declining Urban Areas*, Muller argues that service costs need not increase with annexations, since many annexations recapture fleeing middle-class citizens in neighborhoods that do not use city services proportionally to those in the core city (p. 76). The exception, however, was the Fire Department, which observation is supported by the case study.

8. Muller, ibid., argues that annexations are frequently made to recapture escaping population. This is different from two other more commonly cited functions of annexations, to provide for future growth (in which annexation precedes population) or to accommodate outward pressure of increasing population.

9. On class politics, see Banfield and Wilson, *City Politics*.

10. The relationship between ethnic group antagonism and neighborhood tipping points has often been discussed in the literature. Two examples are Eleanor Wolf, "The Tipping Point in Racially Changing Neighborhoods," *Journal of the American Institute of Planners* 29 (August 1963): 217–222: and P. F. Cressey, "Population Succession in Chicago, 1898–1930," in *Urban Social Segregation*, edited by Ceri Peach (London: Longman, 1975).

11. For the relationship between increase in percentage of blacks and in-

crease in police expenditures, see Henry Terrell, "The Fiscal Impact of Non-whites," in Hirsch et al., *Fiscal Pressures*, esp. pp. 189–191.

12. Daniel Fusfeld, in the *Basic Economics of the Urban Racial Crisis* (New York: Holt, Rinehart and Winston, 1973), pp. 21–22, argues that this experience was typical for blacks coming north at this time. He based the analysis on the work of Charles Killingsworth, *Jobs and Incomes for Negroes* (Ann Arbor: Institute of Labor and Industrial Relations, University of Michigan, 1968).

13. The office was funded out of local revenues until 1978, when it was placed under the Community Development Block Grant.

14. The pattern of other cities' responses to riots has been the subject of several studies. James Button, in *Black Violence: The Political Impact of the 1960s Riots* (Princeton: Princeton University Press, 1979), surveys the responses of several federal departments to riots and suggests that especially for the earlier riots the federal response was to pour more money into riot cities. Later (after 1968) more of a law-and-order emphasis prevailed, especially in the Justice Department. Susan Welch did a multivariate study of cities with over fifty thousand in population and found substantially higher increments in police expenditures in riot cities than in nonriot cities, which suggested a general white blacklash. When city characteristics were controlled, there was no significant difference in social programs; the major impact was on police. See her "Impact of Urban Riots on Urban Expenditures," *American Journal of Political Science* 19 (November 1975): 741–760.

Chapter 4

1. A good description of the intention of reformers in creating the city manager form is in John Porter East's book, *Council Manager Government: The Political Thought of its Founder, Richard S. Childs* (Chapel Hill: University of North Carolina Press, 1965).

2. Two books which discuss the failure of the city manager system to divide policy and administration are Gladys Kammerer, Charles Farris, John DeGrove, and Alfred Clubox, *City Managers in Politics: An Analysis of Manager Tenure and Termination* (Gainesville: University of Florida Monograph Series, Social Sciences A13, University of Florida Press, 1962); and Ronald Loveridge, *City Managers in Legislative Politics* (Indianapolis: Bobbs-Merrill, 1971).

3. The establishment of the Police and Fire Board was mandated by state statute, but because the city had home rule, it could have made changes in that structure. The lack of any personnel policy outside police and fire seems to have been entirely due to the city rather than state mandates.

4. A similar observation was made by Frank Thompson, describing Oakland's personnel policy. See his *Personnel Policy in the City* (Berkeley: University of California Press, 1975).

5. The city manager expressed his fear of losing his job in an interview several months before he was fired.

Chapter 5

1. For an extended discussion on the behavior of city councils, see Heinz Eulau and Kenneth Prewitt, *Labyrinths of Democracy: Adaptations, Linkages, Representation and Policies in Urban Politics* (Indianapolis: Bobbs Merrill, 1973). Also see Irene Rubin, "An Anthropological View of the City Council," in *Proceedings of the First Annual Conference on the Small City and Regional Community*, Stevens Point, Wis.: University of Wisconsin, 1978.

2. Universalism means treating all persons and all cases which have the same characteristics in the same way; particularism means special treatment for some for reasons not intrinsic to the case.

3. There have been many attempts in the literature to typologize political cultural beliefs at the city level, and most of these typologies capture some elements of reform and nonreformed government. See, for example, Daniel Elazar, *Cities of the Prairie: The Metropolitan Frontier and American Politics* (New York: Basic Books, 1970); James Q. Wilson and Edward Banfield, "Public Regardingness as a Value Premise in Voting Behavior," *American Political Science Review* 58 (December 1964): 876–887; and Heinz Eulau and Robert Eyestone, "Policy Maps of City Councils and Policy Outcomes: A Developmental Analysis," *American Political Science Review* 67 (March 1968): 124–143. The idea of deducing the role conceptions from council conflicts was suggested to me by Terry Clark.

4. For Harvey Molotch, the "bricks and mortar syndrome" is indicative of a larger prodevelopmental stance that is tied in with property ownership. See "The City as a Growth Machine: Toward a Political Economy of Place," *American Journal of Sociology* 82 (1977): 309–332. In Southside, there did not appear to be any linkages between classes, as defined by property ownership, and a pro- or anticonstruction stance. More narrowly, however, owners of building supply businesses may have been more proconstruction than funeral directors.

5. Many other authors have listed the resources political actors use. For example, Terry Clark, relying on earlier studies, developed a broad list of resources usable by any actor in the political system, and applied a game theory approach to the translation of resources into influence; see Terry Clark, "The Concept of Power," in Terry Clark, ed., *Community Structure and Decision-Making: Comparative Analyses* (Scranton, Pa.: Chandler, 1968). A somewhat different approach is reported in Richard Frost, "Stability and Change in Local Politics," *Public Opinion Quarterly* 25 (Summer 1961): 221–235. Frost asked politicians how often they performed certain services for constituents. The approach to listing resources used in the present study lies between these extremes of broadness and narrowness. It addresses the question of resources from the point of view of the mayor and council (not from all the political actors) and asks what resources they have to use with all political actors, not just their constituents.

6. A similar point is argued in the literature, namely that the absence of

party and district elections in city manager governments makes them more open to pressure groups, especially unions, than machine governments are. See for example, Alana Northrup and William Dutton, "Municipal Reform in Group Influence," *American Journal of Political Science* 22 (August 1978): 691–711; and David Rogers, *The Management of Big Cities: Interest Groups and Social Change Strategies* (Beverly Hills: Sage, 1971). This argument assumes, however, that politicians want to be reelected and are not serving out of a sense of citizen obligation. Personal political ambition is a characteristic of nonreformed governments. Thus, it is not the pure city manager form which creates vulnerability to interest groups but the compromise between reform and nonreform.

7. The general issue of budgeting as a political process is discussed by many authors but is most often associated with Aaron Wildavsky, *The Politics of the Budgetary Process*, 2nd ed. (Boston: Little, Brown, 1974). In that book Wildavsky is primarily concerned with the federal budget, but the politics of budget requests and approval are analogous in cities.

8. Several other studies have dealt with actual patterns of budgeting in cities as opposed to idealized models. Lewis B. Friedman, in *Budgeting Municipal Expenditures* (New York: Praeger, 1975), provides a good summary of the literature. See also Thomas Anton, *Budgeting in Three Illinois Cities*, (Urbana: Institute of Government and Public Affairs, University of Illinois Press, 1964); and James Danziger, *Making Budgets: Public Resource Allocation* (Beverly Hills: Sage, 1978).

Chapter 6

1. A number of studies have attempted to determine the effect of inflation on urban fiscal crises. These studies have concluded that inflation contributed to fiscal stress but was not an inevitable or uncontrollable cause. In "The Effects of Inflation on Local Government Expenditures," *National Tax Journal* 27 (December 1974): 583–598, David Greytak, Richard Gustely, and Robert Dinklemeyer conclude that while in New York City inflation was severe, nevertheless there was considerable actual growth in goods and services purchased during the period in which fiscal problems developed. Another study of the impacts of inflation was done by Waltzer and Stratton, "Inflation and Municipal Expenditure Increases." This study is most relevant here, since it was based on twenty-four middle-sized cities in Illinois, all comparable to Southside. The authors attribute total increases in expenditures in the median city between 1969–1976 as follows: 30.6% to inflation, 13.9% to growth in real compensation, and 55.5% to increases in quantities of inputs purchased. A third study relevant here is David Greytak and Bernard Jump, *The Impact of Inflation on the Expenditure and Revenues of Six Local Governments, 1971–1979*, Metropolitan Studies Series (Syracuse: Syracuse University Press, 1975). They conclude that inflation affects the tax base at the same rate as expenditures but that such growth in tax base is often not translated into

revenues or is not translated fast enough to prevent deficits. This problem is political and administrative, not a structural result of inflation.

2. For a small city nearby, the cost of fire trucks increased at about 9.05% a year from 1971 to 1978, while in that same city, salaries of fire fighters increased only 3.88% a year from 1973 to 1978. This comparison suggested that the rate of inflation cited for fire trucks was probably accurate. It also suggested that rates of salary increase might be quite variable and not automatically responsive to inflation.

3. There is an extensive literature on the effect of unions on the management process, on wage and benefit levels, and on fiscal stress more broadly. See, for example, Wellington and Winter, *The Unions and The Cities*; David Stanley, *Managing Local Government under Union Pressure* (Washington, D.C.: The Brookings Institution, 1972); Ashenfelter, "The Effects of Unions"; Ronald Ehrenberg, "Municipal Government Structure, Unionization, and the Wages of Firefighters," *Industrial and Labor Relations Review* 27 (October 1973): 36–48; Ehrenberg and Goldstein, "A Model of Public Sector Wage Determination"; Marc Johnson, *The Effect of Unions on Public Sector Wages: A Review of the Econometric Literature*, Metropolitan Studies Series, Maxwell School of Citizenship and Public Affairs (Syracuse: Syracuse University Press, 1976). Also see Clark et al., "How Many New Yorks."

Chapter 7

1. For a description of the potential negative effects of federal revenue during a period of retrenchment, see Levine and Posner, "The Centralizing Effects of Austerity."

2. In a document put out by the Community Development Department containing the 1977 budget and the evaluation of success in 1976, the following statement appears: "Though Block Grant funds represent a considerable amount of federal money to the city, alone it is inadequate to have any significant impact on the more seriously blighted and disinvested areas of the city." As additional evidence of the limited scope of the rehabilitation effort, from January 1976 to September 1976 eleven homes were rehabilitated.

3. The concept of slack as uncommitted resources available for the use of a dominant coalition of organization members was developed in Richard Cyert and James March, *A Behavioral Theory of the Firm* (Englewood Cliffs, N.J.: Prentice-Hall, 1963). They argue that slack is so desirable that members of the dominant coalition will strive to improve the firm's income in order to create some slack resources. The idea developed here is analogous to that of March and Cyert.

Chapter 8

1. For a history of Oakland's conservatism see Arnold Meltsner and Aaron Wildavsky, "Leave City Budgeting Alone! A Survey, Case Study, and Recom-

mendation for Reform," in *Financing the Metropolis: Public Policy in Urban Economics,* pp. 311–358, John P. Crecine ed., Urban Affairs Annual Reviews, vol. 4 (Beverly Hills: Sage, 1970); for an account of Cincinnati, see Charles H. Levine, Irene Rubin, and George Wolohojian, *Fiscal Stress and The Politics of Retrenchment* (Beverly Hills: Sage, 1981).

2. For a description of the areas of increased cost in New York City, see Gustely, "The Components of Change: Social Services."

3. For the expenditure impacts of riots on cities, see especially Welch, "The Impact of Urban Riots."

4. On the impact of changes in the percentage of blacks on police expenditures, see Hirsch et al. *Fiscal Pressures.*

5. Allen Schick has written on the effect of windfall growth at the federal level. See "Budgetary Adaptations to Resource Scarcity" in *Fiscal Stress and Public Policy,* pp. 113–134, Charles H. Levine and Irene Rubin, eds., Sage Year Books in Politics and Public Policy, vol 9 (Beverly Hills: Sage, 1980).

6. That is not to argue that scholars have not attempted to pinpoint the impact of federal grants such as revenue sharing, but only that they have not yet documented the extent or type of reaction to windfall revenues over a period of time. One recent study, Patrick Larkey's *Evaluating Public Programs: The Impact of General Revenue Sharing on Municipal Government* (Princeton: Princeton University Press, 1979), is essentially a model based on a handful of cases over the first year of revenue sharing. The first year was peculiar, he admitted, because only one half year's funds were to arrive during the fiscal year. The first year's funds might therefore be spent differently from the funds received later. The results provide the kind of generality one would expect on this kind of data base: if the city is already fiscally stressed, the money goes into operating expense; if not, then it may be used for reducing taxes or for operating, capital, or increased surplus.

7. See Levine, Rubin, and Wolohojian, *Fiscal Stress and The Politics of Retrenchment.*

8. Morris Janowitz, *The Last Half Century: Societal Change and Politics in America* (Chicago: University of Chicago Press, 1978), 524ff. The demise of the political party is discussed in Willis D. Hawley, *Nonpartisan Politics and the Case for Party Politics* (New York: Wiley, 1974).

10. See the ACIR report, *City Financial Emergencies,* for a discussion of a sample of cities that got into fiscal stress and how it was handled.

11. For a description of the responses of a number of these cities, see Harold Wolman, "Local Government Strategies to Cope with Fiscal Pressure," in *Fiscal Stress and Public Policy,* pp. 231–248.

12. For a list of recommended budgetary reforms that would help cities achieve the preconditions for self-correction, see Irene Rubin, "Preventing or Eliminating Planned Deficits: Restructuring the Incentives," *Public Administration Review* 40: November/December 1980): 621–626.

Bibliography

Adams, J. R. "Anatomy of a Fiscal Crisis." *Public Interest*, 50 (Winter 1978): 132–137.

Advisory Commission on Intergovernmental Relations. *Federal Grants: Their Effects on State and Local Expenditures, Employment Levels and Wage Rates.* Washington, D.C.: USGPO, 1978.

Advisory Commission on Intergovernmental Relations. *City Financial Emergencies.* Washington, D.C.: USGPO, 1973.

Ahlbrandt, Roger, and Brophy, Paul. *Neighborhood Revitalization: Theory and Practice.* Lexington, Mass.: Lexington Books, 1975.

Alcaly, Roger E., and Mermelstein, David, eds. *The Fiscal Crisis of American Cities.* New York: Vintage, 1977.

Aldrich, Howard E., and Reiss, Albert. "Continuities in the Study of Ecological Succession: Changes in the Race Composition of Neighborhoods and Their Businesses." *American Journal of Sociology* 81 (1976): 846–866.

Allison, Graham. *The Essence of Decision: Explaining the Cuban Missile Crisis.* Boston: Little, Brown, 1971.

Alonso, William. "The Economics of Urban Size." *Papers of the Regional Science Association* 26 (1971): 67–83.

———. "Urban Zero Population Growth." *Daedalus* (Fall 1973): 191–206.

American Enterprise Institute. *The Financial Crisis of Our Cities.* Washington, D.C.: American Enterprise Institute for Public Policy Research, 1975.

Anton, Thomas J. *Budgeting in Three Illinois Cities.* Urbana: The Institute of Government and Public Affairs, University of Illinois Press, 1964.

Aronson, J. R., and King, A. E. "Is There a Fiscal Crisis Outside New York?" *National Tax Journal* 31 (June 1978): 153–163.

Ashenfelter, Orley. "The Effect of Unionization on Wages in the Public Sector: The Case of Firefighters." *Industrial and Labor Relations Review* 24 (January 1971): 191–202.

Bahl, Roy. "Measuring the Creditworthiness of State and Local Governments." *Proceedings of the National Tax Association* (1972) 600–622.

————, ed. *The Fiscal Outlook for Cities: Implications of a National Urban Policy*. Syracuse, New York: Syracuse University Press, 1978.

Bahl, Roy; Campbell, Alan; and Greytak, David. *Taxes, Expenditures, and the Economic Base: Case Study of New York City*. New York: Praeger, 1979.

Bahl, Roy; Campbell, Alan; Greytak, David; Jump, Bernard; and Puryear, David. "The Impact of Economic Base Erosion, Inflation and Employee Compensation Costs on Local Governments." Maxwell School Occasional Paper No. 23, Syracuse, 1975.

Balderston, Frederick E. *Managing Today's University*. San Francisco: Jossey Bass, 1974.

Banfield, Edward, and Wilson, James Q. *City Politics*. Cambridge, Mass.: Harvard University Press and M.I.T. Press, 1963.

Baumol, William J. "Macroeconomics of Unbalanced Growth: The Anatomy of Urban Crises." *American Economic Review* 57 (June 1967): 415–420.

Bish, Robert. "Balancing Benefits and Costs in Local Government Fiscal Decision Making." Paper presented to the American Society for Public Administration, Phoenix, 1978.

Bordcherding, Thomas E., ed. *Budgets and Bureaucrats: The Sources of Government Growth*. Durham, N.C.: Duke University Press, 1977.

Bradford, D. F., and Kalejian, H. "An Econometric Model of Flight to the Suburbs." *Journal of Political Economy* 53 (1975): 195–207.

Buchanan, James. *Public Finance in the Democratic Process*. Chapel Hill: University of North Carolina Press, 1967.

Button, James W. *Black Violence: Political Impact of the 1960s Riots*. Princeton, New Jersey: Princeton University Press, 1979.

Caiden Naomi and Wildavsky, Aaron. *Planning and Budgeting in Poor Countries*. New York: Wiley, 1974.

Campbell, Frank, ed. *The States and the Urban Crisis*. New York: Columbia University Press, 1970.

Clark, Terry. *Community Structure and Decision-Making: Comparative Analyses*. Scranton, Pa.: Chandler, 1968.

————. "The Irish Ethic and the Spirit of Patronage." *Ethnicity* 2 (1975): 305–359.

Clark, Terry and Lorna Ferguson. "Fiscal Strain and Fiscal Health in American Cities—Six Basic Processes." Paper presented at the 1977 meetings of the American Sociological Association.

Clark, Terry, with Lorna Ferguson. *Political Leadership and Urban Fiscal Policy* (tentative title). New York: 20th Century Fund, forthcoming.

Clark, Terry; Rubin, Irene; Pettler, Lynn; and Zimmermann, Erwin. "How Many New Yorks: The New York City Fiscal Crisis in Comparative Perspective." Center for Study of Comparative Community Decision-Making, University of Chicago, 1976. (Mimeographed.)

Cloward, Richard A., and Piven, Frances Fox. *The Politics of Turmoil: Essays on Poverty, Race and the Urban Crisis*. New York: Vintage, 1974.

Controller General of the United States. *Federal Seed Money: More Careful Selection and Application Needed*. Washington, D.C.: General Accounting Office, June 1979.

Croswell, R. "Self-Generating Growth in Public Programs." *Public Choice* 21 (Spring 1975): 91–97.

Crecine, John P., ed. *Financing the Metropolis: Public Policy in Urban Economics.* Urban Affairs Annual Reviews, vol. 4. Beverly Hills: Sage, 1970.

Cressey, P. F. "Population Succession in Chicago 1898–1930." In Ceri Peach, ed. *Urban Social Segregation.* London: Longman Publishers, 1975.

Crider, Robert. "The Impact of Inflation on the State and Local Economy." Academy for Contemporary Problems, Urban and Regional Development Series, no. 5, 1978.

———. "The Impact of Recession on State and Local Finance." Academy for Contemporary Problems, Urban and Regional Development Series, no. 6, 1978.

Cummings, Scott and Briggs, Richard. "Catholic and Jewish Immigrants and American Politics: An Historical Analysis of the Roots of Urban Liberalism." Paper Presented at the meetings of the American Sociological Association, 1976.

Danziger, James. *Making Budgets: Public Resource Allocation.* Beverly Hills: Sage, 1978.

Davis, Otto; Dempster, M.; and Wildavsky, A. "A Theory of the Budgetary Process." *American Political Science Review* 60 (September 1966): 529–547.

Downs, Anthony. *Inside Bureaucracy.* Boston: Little, Brown, 1967.

Dye, Thomas. *Politics in States and Communities.* Englewood Cliffs, N.J.: Prentice-Hall, 1969.

East, John Porter. *Council Manager Government: The Political Thought of Its Founder, Richard S. Childs.* Chapel Hill: University of North Carolina Press, 1965.

Ehrenberg, Ronald. "Municipal Government Structure, Unionization, and the Wages of Firefighters." *Industrial and Labor Relations* 27 (October 1973): 36–48.

Ehrenberg, Ronald, and Goldstein, Gerald. "A Model of Public Sector Wage Determination." *Journal of Urban Economics* 2 (1975): 233–245.

Elazar, Daniel. *Cities of the Prairie: The Metropolitan Frontier and American Politics.* New York: Basic Books, 1970.

Eulau, Heinz, and Prewitt, Kenneth. *Labyrinths of Democracy: Adaptations, Linkages, Representation and Policies in Urban Politics.* Indianapolis: Bobbs-Merrill, 1973.

Eulau, Heinz and Eyestone, Robert, "Policy Maps of City Council and Policy Outcomes: A Developmental Analysis." *American Political Science Review* 67 (March 1968): 124–143.

Fainstein, Susan and Fainstein, Norman. "The Federally Inspired Fiscal Crisis. *Social Science and Modern Society* 13 (May/June 1976): 27–32.

Forrester, S. W. *Urban Dynamics.* Cambridge: M.I.T. Press, 1969.

Friedman, Lewis B. *Budgeting Municipal Expenditure: A Study in Comparative Policy Making.* New York: Praeger, 1975.

Frost, Richard. "Stability and Change in Local Politics." *Public Opinion Quarterly* 25 (Summer 1961): 221–235.

Fry, Brian and Winters, Richard. "The Politics of Redistribution." *American Political Science Review* 64 (June 1970): 508–522.

Fusfeld, Daniel Roland. *Basic Economics of the Urban Crisis*. New York: Holt, Rinehart and Winston, 1973.

Gramlich, Edward. "The New York City Fiscal Crisis: What Happened and What is to be Done?" Paper presented to the American Economic Association, 1975.

Greenberg, Michael and Nicholas Valente. "Recent Economic Trends in the Major Northeastern Metropolises." In *Post-Industrial America*, pp. 77–100. Edited by George Sternlieb and James Hughes. New Brunswick, N.J.: Center for Urban Policy Research, Rutgers, The State University of New Jersey, 1975.

Greene, Kenneth, and Munley, Vincent. "Generating Growth in Public Expenditures: The Role of Employee and Constituent Demand." *Public Finance Quarterly* 7 (January 1979): 92–109.

Greenstein, Fred. "The Changing Pattern of Urban Party Politics." *The Annals of the American Academy of Political and Social Science* 353 (May 1964): 1–13.

Greytak, David; Gustely, Richard; and Dinkelmeyer, Robert. "The Effects of Inflation on Local Government Expenditures." *National Tax Journal* 27 (December 1974): 583–598.

Greytak, David and Jump, Bernard. "Inflation and Local Government Expenditures and Revenues: Method and Case Studies." *Public Finance Quarterly* 5 (July 1977): 275–301.

———. "The Effects of Inflation on State and Local Government Expenditures 1967–1974." Syracuse, New York: Maxwell School Occasional Paper no. 25, 1975.

———. *The Impact of Inflation on the Expenditure and Revenues of Six Local Governments, 1971–1979*. Metropolitan Studies Series. Syracuse: Syracuse University Press, 1975.

Grigsby, W. C. *Housing Markets and Public Policy*. Philadelphia: University of Pennsylvania Press, 1963.

Gustely, Richard. *Municipal Public Employment and Public Expenditure*. Lexington, Mass.: D. C. Heath, 1974.

———. "The Components of Change in New York City Government Labor Costs 1965–1972: Police, Fire and Environmental Protection." Syracuse: Maxwell School Project on Public Finances of New York City, Working Paper no. 4, 1972.

———. "The Components of Change in New York City Government Labor Costs 1965–1972: Social Services, Public Schools, Higher Education." Syracuse: Maxwell School of Citizenship and Public Affairs, Project on Public Finances of New York City, Working Paper no. 6, 1973.

Hale, George, and Douglas, Scott. "The Politics of Budget Execution: Financial Manipulation in State and Local Government." *Administration and Society* 9 (November 1977): 367–378.

Hamer, Andrew. *Industrial Exodus from Central City: Public Policy and the Comparative Costs of Location*. Lexington, Mass.: D.C. Heath, 1973.

Hardy, Bruce Allen. "American Privatism and the Urban Fiscal Crisis of the Interwar Years: A Financial Study." Ph.D. dissertation, Wayne State University, 1977.

Hawley, Willis D. Nonpartisan Politics and the Case for Party Politics. New York: Wiley, 1974.

Hempel, George H. The Postwar Quality of State and Local Debt. National Bureau of Economic Research General Series, no. 54. New York: Columbia University Press, 1971.

Hirsch, Werner; Vincent, Phillip; Terrell, Henry; Shoup, Donald; and Rosett, Arthur. Fiscal Pressures on the Central City: The Impact of Commuters, Nonwhites, and Overlapping Governments. New York: Praeger, 1971.

Inman, Robert. "Dissecting the Urban Crisis: Facts and Counter Facts." National Tax Journal 32 (June 1979): 127–142.

Janowitz, Morris. The Last Half Century: Societal Change and Politics in America. Chicago: University of Chicago Press, 1978.

Johnson, Marc. The Effect of Unions on Public Sector Wages: A Review of the Econometric Literature. Metropolitan Studies Series, Maxwell School of Citizenship and Public Affairs. Syracuse: Syracuse University Press, 1976.

Kammerer, Gladys; Farris, Charles D.; DeGrove, John; and Clubox, Alfred. City Managers in Politics: An Analysis of Manager Tenure and Termination. University of Florida Monograph Series, Social Sciences A13. Gainesville: University of Florida Press, 1962.

Killingsworth, Charles. Jobs and Incomes for Negroes. Ann Arbor: Institute for Labor and Industrial Relations, University of Michigan, 1968.

Kohler, Heinz. Economics and Urban Problems. Lexington, Mass.: D. C. Heath, 1973.

Kornblum, William. Blue Collar Community. Chicago: University of Chicago Press, 1974.

Larkey, Patrick D. Evaluating Public Programs: The Impact of Revenue Sharing on Municipal Government. Princeton: Princeton University Press, 1979.

Levine, Charles H. "Organizational Decline and Cutback Management." Public Administration Review 38 (1978): 316–325.

———. "More on Cutback Management." Public Administration Review 39 (1979): 179–183.

Levine, Charles H., and Posner, Paul. "The Centralizing Effects of Austerity on the Intergovernmental System." Presented at the American Political Science Association meetings, Washington, D.C., 1979.

Levine, Charles H., and Wolohojian, George. "The Management of Fiscal Stress: A Study of Cutback Policies in Six Cities." College Park, Institute for Urban Studies, University of Maryland, 1979. (Typewritten.)

Levine, Charles H., and Rubin, Irene, eds. Fiscal Stress and Public Policy. Sage Yearbooks in Politics and Public Policy, vol. 9. Beverly Hills: Sage, 1980.

Levine, Charles H.; Rubin, Irene; and Wolohojian, George. "Resource Scarcity and the Reform Model: Negative Sum Politics in Cincinnati and Oakland." A Paper presented at the meetings of the American Political Science Association, Washington, D.C., 1980.

————. "Resource Scarcity and the Reform Model: The Management of Retrenchment in Cincinnati and Oakland." *Public Administration Review,* forthcoming.

————. *Fiscal Stress and the Politics of Retrenchment: How Local Governments Manage Resource Scarcity.* Beverly Hills: Sage, 1981.

————. "Preconditions for Managing Organizational Retrenchment: Deficiencies and Adaptations in Public Sector." *Administration and Society,* forthcoming.

Liebert, Roland J. *Disintegration and Political Action: The Changing Functions of City Governments in America.* New York: Academic Press, 1976.

Lineberry, Robert, and Fowler, Edmund P. "Reformism and Public Policies in American Cities." *American Political Science Review* 61 (September 1967): 701–716.

Loveridge, Ronald. *City Managers in Legislative Politics.* Indianapolis: Bobbs-Merrill, 1971.

Lyons, William, and Morgan, David R. "The Impact of Intergovernmental Revenue on City Expenditures." *Journal of Politics* 39 (November 1977): 1088–1097.

McCormick, Mary. "Management of Retrenchment: The City of New York in the 1970s." Ph.D. dissertation, Columbia University, 1978.

Mann, Seymour and Mann, Shelden. "Decision Dynamics and Organizational Characteristics: The AFSCME and NYC District Council 37." Paper delivered at the meetings of the American Political Science Association, 1975, circulated by the Urban Research Center, Department of Urban Affairs, Hunter College, New York.

March, James, and Cyert, Richard. *A Behavioral Theory of the Firm.* Englewood Cliffs, N.J.: Prentice-Hall, 1963.

Meltsner, Arnold. *The Politics of City Revenue.* Berkeley, California: University of California Press, 1971.

Meltsner, Arnold and Wildavsky, Aaron. "Leave City Budgeting Alone: A Survey, Case Study, and Recommendation for Reform." In *Financing the Metropolis: Public Policy in Urban Economics.* Edited by John P. Crecine. Urban Affairs Annual Reviews, vol. 4. Beverly Hills: Sage, 1970.

Meyer, John R., and Quigley, John M., eds. *Local Public Finance and the Fiscal Squeeze: A Case Study.* Cambridge, Mass.: Ballinger, 1977.

Mitnick, Barry. "Deregulation as a Process of Organizational Reduction." *Public Administration Review* 38 (1978): 350–357.

Molotch, Harvey. "The City as a Growth Machine: Toward a Political Economy of Place." *American Journal of Sociology* 82 (1977): 309–332.

Moore, Charles. "The Politics of Urban Violence: Policy Outcomes in Winston-Salem." *Social Science Quarterly* 51 (September 1979): 374–388.

Morris, Charles R. *The Cost of Good Intentions: New York City and the Liberal Experiment.* New York: Norton, 1980.

Muller, Thomas. *Growing and Declining Urban Areas.* Washington, D.C.: Urban Institute, 1975.

Muller, Thomas, and Dawson, Grace. *The Impact of Annexation on City Finances.* Washington, D.C.: Urban Institute, 1973.

Muth, Richard. *Cities and Housing*. Chicago: University of Chicago Press, 1969.

Nathan, Richard P., and Adams, Charles F. *Revenue Sharing: The Second Round*. Washington, D.C.: Brookings Institution, 1977.

————. "Understanding Central City Hardship." *Political Science Quarterly* 91 (Spring 1976) 47–62.

Niskanen, William. *Bureaucracy and Representative Government*. Chicago: Aldine-Atherton, 1971.

Northrup, Alana, and Dutton, William. "Municipal Reform in Group Influence." *American Journal of Political Science* 22 (August 1978): 691–711.

O'Connor, James. *The Fiscal Crisis of the State*. New York: St. Martin's Press, 1973.

Olson, Mancur. "The Principle of 'Fiscal Equivalence': Division of Responsibility among Different Levels of Government." *American Economic Review* 59 (May 1969): 479–487.

Olson, Susan, and Lachman, M. L. *Tax Delinquency in the Inner City*. Lexington, Massachusetts: D.C Heath, 1976.

Ostram, Vincent; Tiebout, Charles; and Warren, Robert. "The Organization of Government in Metropolitan Areas: A Theoretical Inquiry." *American Political Science Review* 55 (December 1961): 831–852.

Ott, Attiat, and Yoo, Jang H. "New York City's Financial Crisis: Can the Trend be Reversed?" Washington, D.C.: American Enterprise Institute for Public Policy Research, 1975.

Peacock, A.T., and Wiseman, J. A. "Approaches to the Analysis of Governmental Expenditure Growth." *Public Finance Quarterly* 7 (January 1979): 3–23.

Rich, Richard. "The Complex Web of Urban Governance: Gossamer or Iron." *American Behavioral Scientist* 24 (November/December 1980): 277–298.

Richardson, Harry. *Urban Economics*. Hinsdale, Ill.: Dryden Press, 1978.

————. *Urban Economics*. Harmondsworth, Middlesex, England: Penguin, 1971.

Rogers, David. *Can Business Management Save the Cities? The Case of New York*. New York: Free Press, 1979.

————. *The Management of Big Cities: Interest Groups and Social Change Strategies*. Beverly Hills: Sage, 1971.

Ross, John, and Calkins, Susannah. "The Economic Stimulus Package at Midstream: The Role of State and Local Government." *Publius* 9 (Winter 1979): 45–66.

Rubin, Irene. "An Anthropological View of the City Council." In the *Proceedings of the First Annual Conference on the Small City and Regional Community*. Stephen's Point, Wis.: University of Wisconsin, 1978.

————. "Extent and Causes of Fiscal Stress." Unpublished paper, 1976.

————. "Retrenchment, Loose Structure, and Adaptability in the University." *Sociology of Education* 52 (October 1979): 211–222.

————. "Municipal Budgeting: an Intervening Process Between Politics and Fiscal Stress." Paper presented at the Conference on Politics of the Small City, Macomb, Ill., 1979.

————. "Politics and Retrenchment in the City." Paper presented at the Midwest Political Science Meetings, Chicago, 1979.

————. "Preventing or Eliminating Planned Deficits: Restructuring the Incentives." *Public Administration Review* 40 (November/December 1980): 621–626.

Rubin, Irene, and Levine, Charles H. "State Targeting on Local Fiscal Problems: A View from Below." *The Urban Interest* (December 1981).

Rust, Edgar. *No Growth: Impacts on Metropolitan Areas.* Lexington, Mass.: D.C. Heath, 1975.

Salancik, G., and Pfeffer, J. "Constraints on Administrator Discretion: The Limited Influence of Mayors on City Budgets." *Urban Affairs Quarterly* 12 (June 1977): 475–498.

Schick, Allen. "Budgetary Adaptations to Resource Scarcity." In *Fiscal Stress and Public Policy*, pp. 113–134. Edited by Charles Levine and Irene Rubin. Sage Yearbook in Politics and Public Policy, vol. 9. Beverly Hills: Sage, 1980.

Schmenner, Roger. "The Determination of Municipal Employee Wages." *Review of Economics and Statistics* 55 (1973): 83–90.

Shefter, Martin. "New York City's Fiscal Crisis: The Politics of Inflation and Retrenchment." *The Public Interest* 48 (Summer 1977): 99–127.

Stanley, David. *Managing Local Government Under Union Pressure.* Washington, D.C.: The Brookings Institution, 1972.

Sternlieb, George, and Hughes, James, eds. *Post Industrial America: Metropolitan Decline and Interregional Job Shifts.* New Brunswick, N.J.: Center for Urban Policy Research, Rutgers, The State University of New Jersey, 1975.

Sternlieb, George, and Lake, Robert. "The Dynamics of Real Estate Tax Delinquency." *National Tax Journal* 29 (September 1976): 261–271.

Stinson, Thomas. "Population Changes and Shifts in Local Government Finance." *Municipal Finance* 42 (February 1970): 134–139.

Teune, Henry. "Macro-Theoretical Approaches to Public Policy Analysis: The Fiscal Crisis of American Cities." *Annals of the American Academy of Political and Social Science* 434 (November 1977): 174–185.

Thompson, Frank J. *Personnel Policy in the City.* Berkeley: University of California Press, 1975.

Thompson, Wilbur. *A Preface to Urban Economics: Toward a Conceptual Framework for Study and Research.* Washington: Resources for the Future, 1963.

————. "Economic Processes and Employment Problems in Declining Metropolitan Areas" in *Post-Industrial America*, pp. 187–196. Edited by George Sternlieb and James Hughes. New Brunswick, N.J.: Center for Urban Policy Research, Rutgers, The State University of New Jersey, 1975.

Touche-Ross and Co. *Urban Stress: A Comparative Analysis of 66 U.S. Cities.* New York: Touche-Ross, 1979.

Tullock, Gordon. Review of *Bureaucracy and Representative Government*, by William Niskanen. *Public Choice* 12 (Spring 1972): 119–124.

United States Congress, Congressional Budget Office. "New York City's Fiscal Problem: Its Origin, Potential Repercussions and Some Alternative Policy Responses." Washington, D.C.: USGPO, October, 1975.

United States Congress, Subcommittee on the City of the Committee on Banking Finance and Urban Affairs, 195th Congress, First Session. "How Can Cities Grow Old Gracefully?" Washington, D.C.: USGPO, December 1977.

Waltzer, Norman, and Beveridge, David. Expenditures for Fringe Benefits. Macomb, Ill.: Cities and Villages Municipal Problems Commission, 1976.

Waltzer, Norman, and Stratton, Peter. "Inflation and Municipal Expenditure Increases in Illinois." Macomb, Ill.: Illinois Cities and Villages Municipal Problems Commission, Public Policy Research Institute, Western Illinois University, 1977.

Welch, Susan. "The Impact of Urban Riots on Urban Expenditures." American Journal of Political Science 19 (November 1975): 741–760.

Wellington, Harry, and Winter, Ralph K. The Unions and the Cities. Washington D.C.: The Brookings Institution, 1971.

Whetten, David A. "Organizational Decline: Surfacing an Important Research Topic." College of Commerce and Business Administration, University of Illinois, August 1979. (Typewritten.)

Wildavsky, Aaron. The Politics of the Budgetary Process. 2nd ed. Boston: Little, Brown, 1964.

Williams, Oliver, and Adrian, Charles. Four Cities. Philadelphia: University of Pennsylvania Press, 1963.

Wilson, James Q. Negro Politics. New York: The Free Press, 1960.

Wilson, James Q., and Banfield, Edward. "Public Regardingness as a Value Premise in Voting Behavior." American Political Science Review 58 (December 1964): 876–887.

Wolf, Eleanor. "The Tipping Point in Racially Changing Neighborhoods." Journal of the American Institute of Planners 29 (August 1963): 217–222.

Wolfinger, Raymond. The Politics of Progress. Englewood Cliffs, N.J.: Prentice-Hall, 1974.

Wolfinger, Raymond. "Why Machines Have Not Withered Away and Other Revisionist Thoughts." Journal of Politics 34 (May 1972): 365–398.

Wolfinger, Raymond and Field, John Osgood. "Political Ethos and the Structure of City Government." In Community Structure and Decision-Making: Comparative Analyses, pp. 159–196. Edited by Terry Clark, Scranton, Pa.: Chandler, 1968.

Wolman, Harold. "Local Government Strategies to Cope with Fiscal Pressure." Fiscal Stress and Public Policy, pp. 231–248. Edited by Charles Levine and Irene Rubin. Sage Yearbooks in Politics and Public Policy, vol. 9. Beverly Hills: Sage, 1980.

Yin, Robert K. Changing Urban Bureaucracies: How New Practices Become Routinized. Santa Monica, Cal.: Rand Corporation, 1978.

Young, James, and Breuer, Betty, "Strikes by State and Local Government Employees." Industrial Relations: A Journal of Economy and Society 9 (May 1970): 356–361.

Index